Healthy Leaders

SpiritBuilt Leadership 2

Malcolm Webber

Published by:

Strategic Press
www.StrategicPress.org

Strategic Press is a division of Strategic Global Assistance, Inc.
www.sgai.org

513 S. Main St. Suite 2
Elkhart, IN 46516
U.S.A.

+1-844-532-3371 (LEADER-1)

ISBN 978-1-888810-62-2

All Scripture references are from the New International Version of the Bible, unless otherwise noted.

Printed in the United States of America

Table of Contents

Introduction

This book introduces a new model of Christian leadership. This model describes what constitutes a healthy leader – a holistic leader, a connected leader.

In our churches and Christian ministries, we have many leaders who are "disconnected" from reality. The following are some examples of disconnections:

- The preacher who preaches about knowing God but has no prayer life to speak of. The average American pastor spends about 22 minutes a day in prayer, according to one study. That is a "disconnection."[1]
- The Christian musician who sings that "Jesus is the answer to every problem." Yet he's having an affair with another well-known singer and his marriage is falling apart.
- The evangelist who says he is "building the church of Jesus," yet is not himself committed to any local church.
- The small group leader in a local church who has been saved for many years and has many responsibilities but has never led anyone to the Lord.
- The pastor who is outwardly serving God and building His Kingdom, but inwardly driven by competition with other local pastors.
- The teacher of the Word of God who promotes community life but splits another church to get his own following.
- The leader who genuinely loves God and His people and who tries

---

[1] In South Korea, the average is about 90 minutes a day. In some parts of China, it's probably 2-3 hours a day. Then we wonder why they have revival and we don't!

7

hard but fails due to a lack of competencies.

Disconnections do not necessarily involve sin – although often they will – but they are clear breaches of the way that things should be. Disconnections lead to breakdown and heartbreak. Sometimes the disconnections are so obvious that people outside the church community look at the church and point them out, usually with ridicule.

This new model of leadership is called "ConneXions." Its purpose is to enable a Christian leader to have reality in his life. It is a model of holistic leadership – leadership that is no longer disconnected. It is a model of leadership reality. The word ConneXions has an x in the middle to represent for the Greek letter "chi" which stands for Christ – in the middle. ConneXions is a model of Christ-centered holistic leadership.

The ConneXions model shows us what a healthy leader is, the areas of his life that need to be in order, and how those areas fit together.

Chapter 1

The ConneXions Model of Healthy Leadership

An effective leader possesses a blend of three special elements:

1. Vision. In Christian circles, we could also call this "Calling."
2. Character.
3. Competencies.

All three elements are found in the description of King David in Psalm 78:

> *He chose David his servant and took him from the sheep pens; from tending the sheep he brought him to be the shepherd of his people Jacob, of Israel his inheritance. And David shepherded them with integrity of heart; with skillful hands he led them. (Ps. 78:70-72)*

Verses 70-71 reveal David's calling:

> *He chose David his servant and took him from the sheep pens; from tending the sheep he brought him to be the shepherd of his people*

Verse 72a shows his character:

> *David shepherded them with integrity of heart*

Verse 72b describes David's competencies:

> *with skillful hands he led them.*

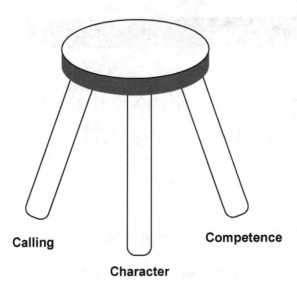

Calling   **Competence**

Character

Just as a stool has three legs, there are three foundations of effective leadership. All three must be *present* and in *balance* for the leader to succeed. The three foundations are calling, character and competencies.

What would happen if one element were missing in the life of a leader?

1. If a leader possessed a strong *calling* and strong *character* but had weak *competencies*, he would produce a big mess! There would be lots of great ideas, good intentions, passion, zeal, sincerity and godliness, but nothing much actually accomplished by the organization.
2. If the leader had strong *character* and strong *competencies*, but was weak in the area of *calling* and vision, the organization would run like a well-oiled machine, but it would not accomplish anything of significant value.
3. To think of a leader with a strong *calling* and strong *competencies*, but who was weak in *character* is the very worst scenario! This combination would spell inevitable disaster for the leader and for everyone in the organization. In the words of Howard Hendricks, "The greatest crisis today is a crisis of leadership. And the greatest peril of leadership

is a crisis of character. Think about it, to give a person management techniques and leadership skills without integrity is simply to enable him to become a better rip-off artist."

We need all three. Thus, the three necessary capacities of effective leadership are character, calling and competencies.

But is this sufficient? Is this model sufficient to describe a mature, balanced and effective Christian leader? Is there anything missing?

There are two elements missing in our model: Christ and Community. These are the two great commandments Jesus gave us:

> One of them, an expert in the law, tested him with this question: "Teacher, which is the greatest commandment in the Law?" Jesus replied: "'Love the Lord your God with all your heart and with all your soul and with all your mind.' This is the first and greatest commandment. And the second is like it: 'Love your neighbor as yourself.' All the Law and the Prophets hang on these two commandments." (Matt. 22:35-40)

The leader must be in right relationship with God and with his brothers.

So, there are actually five elements that must be present in the life of a healthy Christian leader: Calling, Character, Competencies, Christ and Community.

Now, let's put these five in order. Which should come first? Of these five, which produces which?

Here is the order. Our model of the holistic Christian leader starts with his personal relationship with Jesus Christ. The leader must know God.

Christ *must* come first.

> *For no one can lay any foundation other than the one already laid, which is Jesus Christ. (1 Cor. 3:11)*

> *And he is the head of the body, the church; he is the beginning and the firstborn from among the dead, so that in everything he might have the supremacy. (Col. 1:18)*

True leadership is not possible without Christ first! Without Christ first, the other four elements will not work – like a body without a head!

Without Christ first in the life of the leader, he will never get along in community with others:

> *At one time we too were foolish, disobedient, deceived and enslaved by all kinds of passions and pleasures. We lived in malice and envy, being hated and hating one another. (Tit. 3:3)*

Without Christ first, the leader's character will be sinful:

> *So I tell you this, and insist on it in the Lord, that you must no longer live as the Gentiles do, in the futility of their thinking. They are darkened in their understanding and separated from the life of God because of the ignorance that is in them due to the hardening of their hearts. Having lost all sensitivity, they have given themselves over to sensuality so as to indulge in every kind of impurity, with a continual lust for more. (Eph. 4:17-19)*

 Biblically, Christian leadership is not character-based; it is Christ-based. While character is vitally important in Christian leadership, it is not first. Christ is first!

In Christian leadership, everything does not proceed from character and values; everything proceeds from union with Christ. This is not mere semantics but it goes to the very heart of how we understand the Christian life and Christian leadership.

To make this distinction is not to undermine the importance of character and values. On the contrary, this actually establishes true character and values, proceeding not from human effort but from the indwelling life of Christ!

> *...If a man abides in me and I in him, he will bear much fruit...* *(John 15:5)*

> *so that you may be... filled with the fruit of righteousness that comes through Jesus Christ – to the glory and praise of God. (Phil. 1:10-11)*

Without Christ first, the leader will have no calling other than hopelessness and futility:

> *remember that at that time you were separate from Christ, excluded from citizenship in Israel and foreigners to the covenants of the promise, without hope and without God in the world. (Eph. 2:12)*

Sadly, many Christian leaders put their callings first and then try to *use* Christ to fulfill their own ambitious, self-centered visions. But He will not accept second place in anyone's life. We should not pray for power without first praying to know Christ. We should not use the Word of God for teaching, without first using His Word to know Him. Ministry must not be first; in all things, Christ must have the preeminence.

Finally, man's competencies are useless apart from Christ. Without Christ first, the leader is capable of nothing of any value in God's eyes:

> *All of us have become like one who is unclean, and all our righteous acts are like filthy rags... (Is. 64:6)*

> *I am the vine; you are the branches. If a man abides in me and I in him, he will bear much fruit; apart from me you can do nothing. (John 15:5)*

True competencies come from Him:

Not that we are competent in ourselves to claim anything for ourselves, but our competence comes from God. He has made us competent as ministers of a new covenant... (2 Cor. 3:5-6)

Christ must be first! The leader *must* know God. He must walk with God, and out of his relationship with Jesus will proceed every other aspect of his leadership.

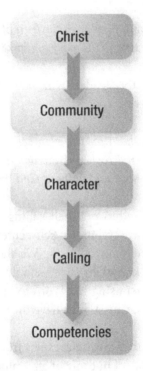

This is not just the "best" way; it is the *only* way to true Christian leadership. Everything else is mere fleshly works.

Second, the leader's personal relationship with Jesus must be expressed and worked out in the daily life of his various communities: his family, his church community, the teams he is a part of, and the broader community of the world.

In this context of Christ and community, character will be formed in the life of the leader. The indwelling life of Christ expressed and worked out in community will develop godly character.

Since God now has someone with character, He can trust him with a calling. Once the leader has a calling he will need the competencies to fulfill that calling.

This is the logical progression of the elements in our model of healthy Christian leadership:

Leaders with wrong priorities will never be satisfied and all they will ever produce will be like filthy rags in God's eyes (Is. 64:6), useless works of wood, hay and stubble:

> For no one can lay any foundation other than the one already laid, which is Jesus Christ. If any man builds on this foundation using gold, silver, costly stones, wood, hay or straw, his work will be shown for what it is, because the Day will bring it to light. It will be revealed with fire, and the fire will test the quality of each man's work. (1 Cor. 3:11-13)

The foundation must be right, and then the building on that foundation must be right. The four elements all come from Christ.

If men put community first, a shallow, humanistic social club will result. If character is put first, legalism and self-righteousness will result. If leaders put calling first, competition and gift-identification will result.

If competencies are put first, self-reliance and mere human achievement will be the results; the leaders may outwardly succeed, but such success will be empty and transient.

Leaders with the wrong first priority will never be satisfied. Moreover, they will always be insecure in their leadership because only Christ brings true security. Insecure leaders, sadly, often become abusive leaders, using others to build their own value and meaning.[2]

That is the logical progression of these elements of healthy Christian leadership. But we should not think that we must address each of these sequentially – as if a leader must first be mature in Christ before he begins to address his need for community, etc. The leader should grow in all five areas concurrently. Consequently, the following is a better way to visualize the relationships of these five elements:

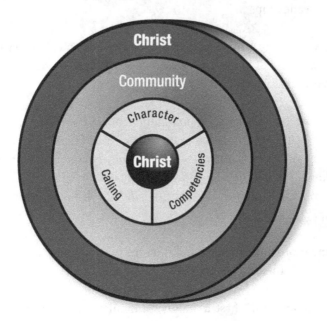

Christ and community are the *contexts* of the healthy leader: he needs to live in Christ and in community. Character, calling and competencies are his *capacities*: they need to be in him.

---

[2] Please see *Abusive Leadership: SpiritBuilt Leadership 6* by Malcolm Webber for more on this.

Christ is the Source of character, calling and competencies. Christ is also the broader context of true community. Truly, He is the Center and Circumference of all things (Eph. 4:4-6)! In community, character is formed, vision is clarified and competencies are developed.[3]

We will now deal with each element of the model in detail.

---

[3] This way of conceptualizing the model also points out a significant difference between the 5C model and the "Be, Know, Do" model that is commonly used in Christian leader development: who we are *in ourselves* (our character, knowledge, and skills) is nowhere near as foundational or important as who we are *in Christ and in community*. Thus, the "Be, Know, Do" model – while a considerable improvement over the traditional academic-only focus of many seminaries – does not give sufficient attention to the centrality and preeminence of the Person of Christ and the importance of community in the life and ministry of the Christian leader.

chapter 2

Christ

In the beginning was the Word, and the Word was with God, and the Word was God. (John 1:1)

"In the beginning was the Word..." In the very beginning God simply "was." John did not write "in the beginning became the Word," because the Eternal Son of God never "became." He always "was" – He eternally "was." God possesses absolute existence, with neither beginning nor end.

But what was God doing "in the beginning" – before anything that we now know existed? What was the nature of this existence of infinite God that it fulfilled, satisfied and delighted Him, not just for a million years, but from eternity, before time itself was even created?

The answer is found in John 1:1:

In the beginning was the Word, and the Word was with God, and the Word was God.

John wrote "the Word was with God." "The Word" is, of course, the Pre-incarnate Son of God (see verse 14). The Son of God was "with" His Father. This tells us something very precious about the eternal nature of the Godhead.

Here in John's Gospel, before he mentions the eternal holiness, love, and truth of God, he writes "the Word was with God." We can learn a simple but life-changing truth here – a truth that gives us profound insight into the nature of Christian leadership.

The meaning of this expression "the Word was with God" is not brought out well in the English translation, where the Greek preposition "pros" is translated as "with."

"Pros," in its usage here, actually means "to," or "toward." In Greek, this preposition can denote motion in a direction toward a thing (when used with an active verb), but here it expresses a position or state looking toward or facing a thing (when used with the verb "to be," as here).

The Word was always *turned toward* God. The Son of God was dwelling "with" His Father; but more than that: He was "turned toward" His Father. In the beginning, before the creation of anything, the Son of God was "with" God, "turned toward" God.

One Greek expositor has written concerning this verse: "Pros implies not merely existence alongside of, but intimate, personal communication." Or, fellowship.

So here we have some insight into the eternal activity of God: fellowship, communion within the Godhead.

What did God do for eternity? What was it that satisfied Him? Fellowship. Fellowship within the Godhead.

John wrote that Jesus "is in the bosom of the Father" (John 1:18). This means that the Son of God is one with His Father – but more than that. It is more than a theological statement about the essential Deity of Christ, and His equality and oneness of being with His Father. The expression implies love, fellowship, intimacy, mutual communion. Jesus is, and always has been, in the bosom of His Father!

There was fellowship within the Godhead for eternity, before the world; and there will be fellowship within the Godhead for eternity when time is no more.

This is the eternal nature of God. God is *fellowship*.

You may never have read this in a "systematic theology," but it is true nevertheless: *The Divine nature is fellowship*. Fellowship is an eternal attribute of God. Just as much as God is eternal, immutable, omnipresent, omniscient, omnipotent and infinite, so God is fellowship. Just as much as God is holy, righteous, truthful, faithful, patient, gracious and merciful, so God's nature is fellowship.

Just as God is light, so God is fellowship. Just as God is love, so God is fellowship. Just as God is glorious, so God is fellowship.

There was never a time when God was not Triune, and there was never a time when God was not active; so there was never a time when God was not fellowshipping within Himself. Fellowship is the eternal nature, activity and very essence of God. T*his is what God was doing in eternity!*

In the beginning was the Son of God, and the Son of God was with His Father. He was "toward" His Father, looking at Him, communing with Him in loving, joyful, spontaneous, abundant fellowship. [4]

Before the creation of the world, the Godhead was highly active. For eternity, there was fellowship within the Godhead, between the Father, the Son and the Holy Spirit.

This is the eternal nature of God. God's nature is fellowship. This is who God is. He is a God of fellowship. He is a God of loving, joyful, spontaneous, delighted communion.

When God created man, He made man to experience this life – to experience this fellowship. When man sinned, he lost his relationship with God; he lost the presence of God. But Jesus came to the earth to die on the cross that man might be restored to God: to His fellowship, to His presence.

---

[4] For a detailed study of this awesome truth, please see *In Him Was Life* by Malcolm Webber.

This is where we find life – in eternity – in Him, in His fellowship. Life, and all that life produces – faith, holiness, righteousness, love, the fruits and gifts of the Spirit, church life and leadership – are only found in Him, in His fellowship.

> *Now this is eternal life: that they may know you, the only true God, and Jesus Christ, whom you have sent. (John 17:3)*

Fellowship is the very life of God. It is the eternal nature and infinite being of God. It is the very essence and heart of the Godhead. Fellowship is not just something God does in His spare time, when He has nothing better to do. It is not something He does once a week on Sunday morning. Fellowship is what He *is*. Fellowship is the eternal nature of God. It is His being.

In eternity was God, and in Him was fellowship. God did not purpose to keep this life to Himself; and He has invited *us* to participate in His fellowship – in this same fellowship of the Godhead!

> *We proclaim to you what we have seen and heard, so that you also may have fellowship with us. And our fellowship is with the Father and with his Son, Jesus Christ. (1 John 1:3)*

This is what the Christian life is: participation in the joyful, delighted, spontaneous, eternal fellowship of the Godhead! And this is where Christian leadership comes from – fellowship with God!

During His ministry on the earth, Jesus lived the same way that He had always lived – in fellowship with His Father. Jesus lived the same way He did before creation. The Word was "toward" God. The Word was beholding God, in joyful, loving, delighted fellowship with Him. This inward fellowship was the source of all His leadership.

During His earthly ministry, Jesus lived in continuous fellowship with His Father.

The one who sent me is with me... (John 8:29)

He was fully and inwardly submitted to His Father's will:

> *For I have come down from heaven not to do my will but to do the will of him who sent me. (John 6:38)*

> *...I love the Father and... I do exactly what my Father has commanded me... (John 14:31)*

This inward, spiritual fellowship was the source of everything in His life and ministry. By this inward life, Jesus overcame all temptation (Heb. 4:15; Luke 4:1-13; Matt. 26:39) and loved others to the point of complete self-giving (Phil. 2:5-11).

This inward fellowship was the source of all His words:

> *The Jews were amazed and asked, "How did this man get such learning without having studied?" Jesus answered, "My teaching is not my own. It comes from him who sent me..." (John 7:15-16)*

> *...what I have heard from him I tell the world...I do nothing on my own but speak just what the Father has taught me. The one who sent me is with me; he has not left me alone, for I always do what pleases him. (John 8:26-29)*

> *For the one whom God has sent speaks the words of God, for God gives the Spirit without limit. (John 3:34)*

> *I am telling you what I have seen in the Father's presence...(I have) told you the truth that I heard from God... (John 8:38-40)*

> *For I did not speak of my own accord, but the Father who sent me commanded me what to say and how to say it. I know that his command leads to eternal life. So whatever I say is just what the Father has told me to say. (John 12:49-50)*

...These words you hear are not my own; they belong to the Father who sent me. (John 14:24)

...I gave them the words you gave me... (John 17:8)

This was why Jesus could respond to complicated challenges with merely a few perfect words that silenced all His opposers (e.g., Matt. 22:29-32; Mark 12:16-17; John 8:7). This was why He could, with just one sentence, get right to the core of deep heart issues (e.g., Luke 18:22; John 4:7-26).

His inward fellowship with His Father was the source of all His works:

...(I) must do the work of him who sent me... (John 9:4)

It was the source of all His wisdom:

By myself I can do nothing; I judge only as I hear... (John 5:30)

But if I do judge, my decisions are right, because I am not alone. I stand with the Father, who sent me. (John 8:16)

It was the source of all His power:

...it is the Father, living in me, who is doing his work. (John 14:10)

...God anointed Jesus of Nazareth with the Holy Spirit and power, and how he went around doing good and healing all who were under the power of the devil, because God was with him. (Acts 10:38)

It was the source of all Jesus' abilities:

...the Son can do nothing by himself; he can do only what he sees his Father doing, because whatever the Father does the Son also does. For the Father loves the Son and shows him all he does. Yes, to your amazement he will show him even greater things than these. (John 5:19-20)

...everything you have given me comes from you. (John 17:7)

Thus Jesus revealed, not simply His own life, but the life and Person of His Father to the world:

> *If you really knew me, you would know my Father as well. From now on, you do know him and have seen him... Anyone who has seen me has seen the Father... (John 14:7-9)*

> *Then Jesus cried out, "When a man believes in me, he does not believe in me only, but in the one who sent me. When he looks at me, he sees the one who sent me."(John 12:44-45)*

> *No one has ever seen God, but God the One and Only, who is at the Father's side, has made him known. (John 1:18)*

> *I have revealed you to those whom you gave me out of the world. They were yours; you gave them to me and they have obeyed your word. Now they know that everything you have given me comes from you. (John 17:6-7)*

This was how Jesus lived His life on the earth. He lived in continuous fellowship with His Father, and through that fellowship He drew from, and lived by, His Father's life. His life was through His fellowship with His Father.

Thus, Jesus' *leadership* came from His union with His Father.

In the relationship between Jesus and His Father, we are going to find a parallel to what our own relationship with God can be.

> *Whoever eats my flesh and drinks my blood abides in me, and I in him. Just as the living Father sent me and I live because of the Father, so the one who feeds on me will live because of me. (John 6:56-57)*

Here Jesus makes a statement about the relationship He had with His

Father while He was upon the earth; and He draws a parallel between that relationship with His Father and our relationship with Him. In these verses, Jesus said that He lived by the life of His Father, and that we are to live by His life in the same way that He lived by His Father.

Jesus didn't just tell us to live the Christian life – or to be Christian leaders – and then leave it up to us to define what that meant and to figure out how to do it. But Jesus showed us what the Christian life and what Christian leadership look like – in His own life. He showed us and told us how to do it: we are to live by His life *in the same way* that He lived by His Father's life.

Just as Jesus lived His life by the life of His Father in Him, so we are to live our Christian lives by the life of Jesus in us.

> *Just as the living Father sent me and I live because of the Father, so (i.e. even so, or in the same manner) the one who feeds on me will live because of me. (John 6:57)*

Just as Jesus lived in continuous fellowship with His Father, so we are to live in constant fellowship with Him by His Spirit.

Jesus' leadership entirely came from His union with His Father, and He sent us to lead the same way (John 20:21).

Jesus gave us a wonderful promise of abiding fellowship with God:

> *… He who loves me will be loved by my Father, and I too will love him and show myself to him…My Father will love him, and we will come to him and make our home with him. (John 14:21-23)*

> *We proclaim to you what we have seen and heard, so that you also may have fellowship with us. And our fellowship is with the Father and with his Son, Jesus Christ. (1 John 1:3)*

We experience this wonderful fellowship with God by His Spirit:

But when he, the Spirit of truth, comes, he will guide you into all truth. He will not speak on his own; he will speak only what he hears, and he will tell you what is yet to come. He will bring glory to me by taking from what is mine and making it known to you. All that belongs to the Father is mine. That is why I said the Spirit will take from what is mine and make it known to you. (John 16:13-15; cf. Luke 10:22)

Jesus looked at the Father and listened to His voice and thus perfectly revealed Him to the world (John 17:10a). The Holy Spirit now looks at the Son and listens to Him and thus reveals the Son of God to us.

Furthermore, as this Divine fellowship was the source of Jesus' words and works – indeed of His entire life, ministry and leadership – so our experience of Divine fellowship will be the source of all true Christian character, fruit and leadership in our lives.

But we all, with unveiled face, beholding as in a mirror the glory of the Lord, are being transformed into the same image from glory to glory, just as by the Spirit of the Lord. (2 Cor. 3:18, NKJV)

I can do everything through him who gives me strength. (Phil. 4:13)

On that day you will realize that I am in my Father, and you are in me, and I am in you. (John 14:20)

...If a man abides in me and I in him, he will bear much fruit; apart from me you can do nothing. (John 15:5)

And we pray this in order that you may live a life worthy of the Lord and may please him in every way: bearing fruit in every good work, growing in the knowledge of God, being strengthened with all power according to his glorious might so that you may have great endurance and patience, and joyfully giving thanks to the Father... (Col. 1:10-12)

So then, just as you received Christ Jesus as Lord, continue to live in him, rooted and built up in him, strengthened in the faith as you were taught, and overflowing with thankfulness. (Col. 2:6-7)

and you have been given fullness in Christ, who is the head over every power and authority. (Col. 2:10)

If you have any encouragement from being united with Christ, if any comfort from his love, if any fellowship with the Spirit, if any tenderness and compassion, (Phil. 2:1)

No, in all these things we are more than conquerors through him who loved us. (Rom. 8:37)

But by the grace of God I am what I am, and his grace to me was not without effect. No, I worked harder than all of them – yet not I, but the grace of God that was with me. (1 Cor. 15:10)

For we do not preach ourselves, but Jesus Christ as Lord, and ourselves as your servants for Jesus' sake. For God, who said, "Let light shine out of darkness," made his light shine in our hearts to give us the light of the knowledge of the glory of God in the face of Christ. But we have this treasure in jars of clay to show that this all-surpassing power is from God and not from us. (2 Cor. 4:5-7)

I have been crucified with Christ and I no longer live, but Christ lives in me. The life I live in the body, I live by faith in the Son of God, who loved me and gave himself for me. (Gal. 2:20)

If anyone speaks, he should do it as one speaking the very words of God. If anyone serves, he should do it with the strength God provides, so that in all things God may be praised through Jesus Christ. To him be the glory and the power for ever and ever. Amen. (1 Pet. 4:11)

His divine power has given us everything we need for life and godliness through our knowledge of him who called us by his own glory and goodness. Through these he has given us his very great and precious promises, so that through them you may participate in the divine nature and escape the corruption in the world caused by evil desires. (2 Pet. 1:3-4)

As a result, just as Jesus, through living by His Father's life, revealed His Father to the world, so we, through living by means of Jesus' indwelling life, will express His life and being to the world. As Paul testified:

...God...was pleased to reveal his Son in me... (Gal. 1:15-16)

For those God foreknew he also predestined to be conformed to the likeness of his Son... (Rom. 8:29)

We always carry around in our body the death of Jesus, so that the life of Jesus may also be revealed in our body. For we who are alive are always being given over to death for Jesus' sake, so that his life may be revealed in our mortal body. So then, death is at work in us, but life is at work in you. (2 Cor. 4:10-12)

until we all reach unity in the faith and in the knowledge of the Son of God and become mature, attaining to the whole measure of the fullness of Christ...speaking the truth in love, we will in all things grow up into him who is the Head, that is, Christ. (Eph. 4:13-15)

I in them and you in me. May they be brought to complete unity to let the world know that you sent me and have loved them even as you have loved me. (John 17:23; see also Matt. 10:20)

No one has ever seen God; but if we love one another, God lives in us and his love is made complete in us. (1 John 4:12)

This is the simple nature of the Christian life: union with Jesus, and living by means of His indwelling life.

Thus, this is the source of Christian leadership: fellowship with Jesus Christ by His indwelling Spirit. It is Divine fellowship that enables us to live and lead according to Divine life.

> *...If a man abides in me and I in him, he will bear much fruit; apart from me you can do nothing. (John 15:5)*

Fellowship is the connection. It is through inward fellowship with God that we partake of His nature (2 Cor. 3:18). It is through His fellowship that He imparts His works, His gifts, His fruits, His endurance, His leadership and Himself to us. It is by His fellowship that He reveals Himself through us. It is by fellowship with God that we live the Christian life and lead as Christian leaders.

It was Jesus' fellowship with His Father, in itself, that enabled Him to live and lead by His Father's life. So it is our fellowship with the Father and the Son, in itself, that will be the source of our life and leadership.

In fellowship with God is life, and is the whole of the Christian life. Jesus said we are to "eat" of Him, to partake of Him, and thus to live by Him. We are to dwell in Him and He in us. We are called to fellowship with Him, to behold Him, to enter into this great eternal activity of the Godhead: this Divine fellowship.

What a privilege! What a calling! And this is the Christian life!

> *Now this is eternal life: that they may know you, the only true God, and Jesus Christ, whom you have sent. (John 17:3)*

This is Christian leadership. It is in Jesus Christ. It is in personal fellowship with Him. It is in His abiding presence.

Christian leadership is only found in Jesus Christ. True leadership is not found in anything other than Him – in anything other than His Person – in anything other than a living, abiding union and fellowship with Him.

Christian leadership starts with Him. Otherwise, it is all worthless.

True leadership begins with Christ. Jesus, Himself, is the Foundation that must be in place in the leader's life. The leader must know God and walk with God in a daily, experienced inward union and fellowship.

Jesus must be the Fountainhead of everything in your life and ministry. It all must proceed from a personal, daily, experiential relationship with the Lord Jesus.

Jesus' disciples led out of their fellowship with Him:

> When they saw the courage of Peter and John and realized that they were unschooled, ordinary men, they were astonished and they took note that these men had been with Jesus. (Acts 4:13)

Although Peter and John were untrained and uneducated men (cf. John 7:15; 2 Cor. 11:6), those around them marveled at their boldness and realized it was because they "had been with Jesus." So it can, and should, be with us!

> Abide in me, and I will abide in you. No branch can bear fruit by itself; it must abide in the vine. Neither can you bear fruit unless you abide in me. I am the vine; you are the branches. If a man abides in me and I in him, he will bear much fruit; apart from me you can do nothing. (John 15:4-5)

Jesus is the vine and we are the branches. Only in Him can we bear leadership-fruit that is pleasing to God.

One of the first things Jesus did with His disciples was to teach them to pray:

> One day Jesus was praying in a certain place. When he finished, one of his disciples said to him, "Lord, teach us to pray, just as John taught his disciples." He said to them, "When you pray, say... (Luke 11:1-2)

Apparently, John the Baptist had done the same with his disciples: he taught them to pray. Relationship with God must be first in a leader's life. Our leadership is an extension of His leadership (1 Pet. 5:2, 4); therefore, our leadership must proceed from union with Him.

A leader who knows God:

- Will trust Him.
- Will be secure in Him. This is so important since leadership is filled with much painful rejection.
- Will have a vibrant prayer life in Him. Jesus' prayer life was vibrant because He knew His Father; Paul's prayer life was powerful because he knew Christ. Out of inward union with Christ comes the leader's prayer life.
- Will love His people as He loves them.
- Will be united with Him in His sufferings, which will produce maturity, brokenness and faith in God.

Too often, unfortunately, Christian leaders are too busy with "ministry stuff" to spend sufficient time developing their inward lives in Christ.

Too many Christians are "familiar" with God and the things of God but they are not intimately united with Him on an ongoing daily basis. Knowing God, however, is not mere familiarity, which often breeds contempt, but genuine union with Him.

The first revelation a Christian leader has should not concern any vision other than the revelation of the Person of Jesus:

> Simon Peter answered, "You are the Christ, the Son of the living God." Jesus replied, "Blessed are you, Simon son of Jonah, for this was not revealed to you by man, but by my Father in heaven." (Matt. 16:16-17)

This revelation of the Person of Jesus Christ will be the foundation for the whole of the leader's life and ministry. All spiritual building must be upon this foundation: the revelation of the Person of Jesus. It is not merely facts about Him or about what He did. The leader must have a life-changing inner revelation about Jesus Himself.

In Jesus' days there were many who followed Him, who even pressed upon Him and were healed, yet they did not "know" Him. They saw Him as a useful answer to some of their own needs, but they did not see Him as the Foundation of their lives and ministries. Similarly, many Christian leaders today try to use Christ to achieve their own ambitions.

The Father is very jealous for His Son. He will not allow any other foundation than the revelation of His Son. Any revelation other than the Person of Jesus will only distract from Him. Any source of leadership other than the Person of Jesus will only waste our time and energy. Jesus is to have the preeminence.

> ...that in all things He may have the preeminence. (Col. 1:18, NKJV)

When a leader builds his inner life in Christ first, then his whole ministry will change. The following are the words of DeVern Fromke[5]:

> ...as Christ is built into the inner fabric it will be evident that only He is material for spiritual building...We must realize that there can never be any greater ministry outwardly than what has been wrought within our inner man...If there is a proper foundation laid in us, then we will produce that foundation in others. If there is a proper spiritual building going up in us, then we will produce that same building in others. Our outward ministry is actually the reflection of our inner life.

---

[5] From *No Other Foundation*, pp. 11-12.

Paul seemed to understand this principle when he wrote to the Corinthians. We have quoted his statement: "I have laid a foundation." Now he continues by saying, "But any man who builds on the foundation using as his material gold, silver, precious stones, wood, hay, stubble, must know that each man's work will one day be shown for what it is" (1 Cor. 3: 10).

God may allow our life-work to stand momentarily, but He will not allow anything which is not proper building material to remain on the foundation. I can almost hear Him saying to some of those who are now building, "You may spend your whole life on that, but it will all go up in smoke. It is not suitable building material; it is not some thing of Christ which I have wrought by the Spirit into lives."

What is this wood, hay and stubble which God will not allow as building material? One may look at pastors who have spent years in gathering people in their congregation. To the visible eye it looks like something has been done. Yet God sees the human energies of man without the help of the Spirit and announces: "This is just a pile of boards. I cannot accept them unless they are overlaid with gold. And this overlaying is not of man, but a work of the Spirit." God is forced to announce: "Have I not told you I cannot have this on my Foundation for it is something wrought of man. It is too earthy. I must have gold which I have wrought through pressure, through fire, through purifying."

Again, we have seen men build knowledge, doctrine, theology into people. Yet in the hour of real pressure all that has not been translated into reality will not hold them. It is like hay and stubble they have been feeding upon, and this can never nourish the inner man nor become building material for God. Recently I heard a brother, who had been an outstanding Bible teacher for 15 years, share the deepest confession of his heart: "All I have known has only puffed me up, but it has not built me up in the inner life. Outwardly I am a builder, but inwardly I am a shambles. I, myself, have been feeding upon mere hay and feeding it to others."

The leader's greatest need is to know the Lord. The following are the words of T. Austin Sparks[6]:

"That I may know..." (Phil. 3:10). "Have I been so long time with you, and dost thou not know Me." (John 14:9, A.S.V.). Phil. 1:10; Heb. 8:11; I John 2:20, 27.

It is of the greatest importance for the Lord's children to recognize fully that, above all other things, His object is that they should know Him. This is the all-governing end of all His dealings with us. This is the greatest of all our needs.

It is the secret of strength, steadfastness, and service. It determines the measure of our usefulness to Him. It was the one passion of the life of the apostle Paul for himself. It was the cause of his unceasing striving for the saints. It is the heart and pivot of the whole letter to the Hebrews. It was the secret of the life, service, endurance, confidence of the Lord Jesus as Son of Man.

All these facts need looking at more closely. We begin always with the Lord Jesus as God's representative, the Man after His own mind. In His life on earth there was no part or aspect which did not have its strength and ability rooted in, and drawn from, His inward knowledge of His Father, God. We must never forget that His was a life of utter dependence upon God, voluntarily accepted. He attributed everything to the Father: word, wisdom, and works. The miracles were made just as possible through His apostles as through Himself. This does not put the apostles on the same personal level as Himself. His Deity remains. He is God manifest in the flesh; but He has accepted from the human and manward standpoint the limitations and dependence of man so that God

---

[6] From *A Witness and a Testimony*, Vol. 49, No. 2.

might be God manifested. There is a subjection here because of which He is able to do nothing of Himself (John 5:19, etc.). The principle of His entire life in every phase and detail was His knowledge of God. He knows the Father in the matter of the words He speaks, the works He does, the men and women with whom He has to do; with regard to the times of speaking, acting, going, staying, surrendering, refusing, silence; with regard to the motives, pretensions, professions, enquiries, suggestions, of men and of Satan. He knows when He may not, and when He may, give His life. Yes, everything here is governed by that inward knowledge of God. There are numerous evidences in the "Acts" as the practical, and in the Epistles as the doctrinal, revelation of God's mind, that this principle is intended by God to be maintained as the basic law of the life of the Lord's people through this age. This knowledge in the case of the Lord Jesus was the secret of His complete ascendancy and of His absolute authority.

Masters in Israel will seek Him out and the issue which will precipitate their seeking will be that of knowing. "Art thou the teacher of Israel, and understandest not these things?" (John 3:10). Nicodemus has come to One Who knows, and Whose authority is superior to that of the scribes, not merely in degree but in kind.

Toward the end of the Gospel of John, which especially brings into view this very matter, "to know" occurs some fifty-five times. Our Lord makes the statement that "this is life eternal, that they should know Thee the only true God, and Him, Whom Thou didst send, even Jesus Christ." (John 17:3). This does not mean merely that eternal life is given on the basis of this knowledge. There can be life with very limited knowledge. But life in fulness is closely related to that knowledge, and the increasing knowledge of Him manifests itself in increasing life. It works both ways; knowledge unto life and life unto knowledge. Seeing, then, that the Lord Jesus Himself, as Man, represents man according to God, we are well prepared to see that *the dominating objective of the divine dealings with us is that we may know the Lord.*

This explains all our experiences, trials, sufferings, perplexities, weakness, predicaments, tight corners, bafflings, pressures. While the refining of spirit, the development of the graces, the removing of the dross, are all purposes of the fires, yet above and through all is the one object - that we may know the Lord. There is only one way of really getting to know the Lord, and that is experimentally.

Our minds are so often occupied with service and work; we think that doing things for the Lord is the chief object of life. We are concerned about our lifework, our ministry. We think of equipment for it in terms of study and knowledge of things. Soul-winning, or teaching believers, or setting people to work, are so much in the foreground. Bible study and knowledge of the Scriptures, with efficiency in the matter of leading in Christian service as the end in view, are matters of pressing importance with all. All well and good, for these are important matters; but, back of everything the Lord is more concerned about our knowing Him than about anything else. It is very possible to have a wonderful grasp of the Scriptures, a comprehensive and intimate familiarity with doctrine; to stand for cardinal verities of the faith; to be an unceasing worker in Christian service; to have a great devotion to the salvation of men, and yet, alas, to have a very inadequate and limited personal knowledge of God within. So often the Lord has to take away our work that we may discover Him. The ultimate value of everything is not the information which we give, not the soundness of our doctrine, not the amount of work that we do, not the measure of truth that we possess, but just the fact that we know the Lord in a deep and mighty way.

This is the one thing that will remain when all else passes. It is this that will make for the permanence of our ministry after we are gone. While we may help others in many ways and by many means so far as their earthly life is concerned, our real service to them is based upon our knowledge of the Lord...

Howard O. Pittman was a Baptist minister for 35 years. [7] On August 3, 1979, his main body trunk artery ruptured and at some point in the following hours, he experienced physical death. His spirit left his body and he was taken before the throne of God where he pleaded for an extension of his physical life. It was here that God showed him what kind of life he had really led. His words follow:

> As I stood before the Gates, the sense of joy, happiness, and contentment radiated out from Heaven. I could feel the warmth it produced and as I stood there to plead my case, I could feel the awesome power of God.

> Boldly I came before the throne and started out by reminding God what a great life of love, worship, and sacrifice I had lived for Him. I told Him of all the works I had done, reminding Him that I had accepted Him when I was quite young and that I had served Him all my life for all these many years. I reminded Him that I was now in trouble and only God could help by granting me an extension of my physical life. God was totally silent while I spoke. When I had completed my request, I heard the real, audible voice of God as God answered me.

> The sound of His voice came down on me from over the Gates even before the words hit me. The tone of His anger knocked me on my face as God proceeded to tell me just what kind of life I had really lived. God told me what God really thought of me and even others who did as I had. God pointed out that my faith was dead, that my works were not acceptable, and that I had labored in vain. God told me that it was an abomination for me to live such a life and then dare call it a life of worship.

> I could not believe God was talking to me in this manner! I had served Him for years! I thought I had lived a life pleasing to Him! As God was enumerating my wrongs, I was sure God had me

---

[7] The following is taken from *Placebo* by Howard Pittman, pp. 32-34.

confused with someone else. There was no strength left in me to even move, let alone protest, yet I was panicking within myself.

No way God could be talking about me! I just could not believe that what God said was referring to me! All of these years I thought I was doing those works for God! Now God was telling me that what I did, I did for myself. Even as I preached and testified about the saving grace of Jesus Christ, I was doing that only for myself in order that my conscience might be soothed. In essence, my first love and first works were for myself. After MY needs and wants were met or satisfied, in order to soothe my conscience I would set out to do the Lord's work. This made my priorities out of order and unacceptable. Actually, I had become my own false god.

He makes it plain in His teachings that He is a jealous God and will have no other gods before Him; flesh, stone, blood, or whatever. He will have no other gods before Him...

Only now as I was here before Him being chastised did...two portions of Scripture become crystal clear to me as to their true meaning:

> *Then Jesus said to his disciples, "If anyone would come after me, he must deny himself and take up his cross and follow me. For whoever wants to save his life will lose it, but whoever loses his life for me will find it. What good will it be for a man if he gains the whole world, yet forfeits his soul? Or what can a man give in exchange for his soul?" (Matt. 16:24-26)*

> *"If anyone comes to me and does not hate his father and mother, his wife and children, his brothers and sisters – yes, even his own life – he cannot be my disciple. And anyone who does not carry his cross and follow me cannot be my disciple... any of you who does not give up every- thing he has cannot be my disciple." (Luke 14:26-33)*

As God told me about my true motives, I could see plainly for the first time how my works were dead. Because God was displaying His wrath toward me, I could not stand nor could I speak. No strength was left within me as I was nothing more than a wet rag lying there writhing in agony.

It needs to be stated that at no time while God was chastising me did God say I was not saved nor did God say that my name was not in the Lamb's Book of Life. God never mentioned salvation to me at all but only spoke about the works produced through my life. God told me the type of life I lived was an unacceptable life for a true Christian. As God spoke to me of my dead works, God indicated that there are some people who are not saved but think they are. These people will experience His everlasting wrath. He also made it plain to me that there are others of His children who will find themselves in my present condition on Judgment Day. This revealed to me the true meaning of 1 Corinthians 3:15 which states, "If any man's work shall be burned, he shall suffer loss: but he himself shall be saved; yet so as by fire."[8]

Jesus came to a friend of mine once and showed her a pile of stinking garbage. It was a heap of garbage and filth, and was absolutely vile and disgusting. She understood that the garbage became viler and viler toward the center of the heap. The Lord told her that all of her most righteous works were worse, far worse, than the vilest, most stinking part of the garbage and filth before her.

All of us have become like one who is unclean, and all our righteous acts are like filthy rags... (Is. 64:6)

Christian leadership that does not proceed first and only from Christ will be completely worthless in the end.

---

[8] Graciously, God brought Pittman back to life and sent him out with a message of preparation for Jesus' soon return.

Unless the LORD builds the house, its builders labor in vain... (Ps. 127:1)

By the grace God has given me, I laid a foundation as an expert builder, and someone else is building on it. But each one should be careful how he builds. For no one can lay any foundation other than the one already laid, which is Jesus Christ. If any man builds on this foundation using gold, silver, costly stones, wood, hay or straw, his work will be shown for what it is, because the Day will bring it to light. It will be revealed with fire, and the fire will test the quality of each man's work. If what he has built survives, he will receive his reward. If it is burned up, he will suffer loss; he himself will be saved, but only as one escaping through the flames. (1 Cor. 3:10-15)

Thus, Christian leadership begins with knowing God personally. Then, we know Him together in the context of the church.

chapter 3

Community

The Christian life is personal union and fellowship with Jesus (John 17:3). Church life is knowing God together. Moreover, together – in the context of the community of believers – we can know God in His fullness.

The following passages, all of which describe the corporate body of Christ, and not merely the life of the individual believer, demonstrate that together the community of believers can experience God in His fullness[9]:

> *The body is a unit, though it is made up of many parts; and though all its parts are many, they form one body. So it is with Christ... Now the body is not made up of one part but of many. (1 Cor. 12:12-14)*

> *in whom you also are being built together for a dwelling place of God in the Spirit. (Eph. 2:22)*

> *I pray that out of his glorious riches he may strengthen you with power through his Spirit in your inner being, so that Christ may dwell in your hearts through faith. And I pray that you, being rooted and established in love, may have power, together with all the saints, to grasp how wide and long and high and deep is the love of Christ, and to know this love that surpasses knowledge – that you may be filled to the measure of all the fullness of God. (Eph. 3:16-19)*

It is not individually but together that we will be filled with His fullness.

---

[9] Please see Chapter 7 in *To Enjoy Him Forever* by Malcolm Webber for more on this.

until we all reach unity in the faith and in the knowledge of the Son of God and become mature, attaining to the whole measure of the fullness of Christ. Then we will no longer be infants, tossed back and forth by the waves, and blown here and there by every wind of teaching and by the cunning and craftiness of men in their deceitful scheming. Instead, speaking the truth in love, we will in all things grow up into him who is the Head, that is, Christ. From him the whole body, joined and held together by every supporting ligament, grows and builds itself up in love, as each part does its work. (Eph. 4:13-16)

and you have been given fullness in Christ, who is the head over every power and authority. (Col. 2:10)

the Head, from whom the whole body, supported and held together by its ligaments and sinews, grows as God causes it to grow. (Col. 2:19)

In the above passages, the promise of the fullness of God is given to the Body of Christ. Spiritual maturity is a corporate experience, not just an individual one. There is only one bride, one temple, one body of Christ. It is together that we know Christ and reveal Him to the world:

A new command I give you: Love one another. As I have loved you, so you must love one another. By this all men will know that you are my disciples, if you love one another. (John 13:34-35)

that all of them may be one, Father, just as you are in me and I am in you. May they also be in us so that the world may believe that you have sent me. (John 17:21)

No one has ever seen God; but if we love one another, God lives in us and his love is made complete in us. (1 John 4:12)

So, in the life of the community, as we love and serve one another, the daily realities of our own walks with Jesus are expressed in our relationships with one another.

The following words are from *In Him Was Life* in a section on the nature of Christian fellowship[10]:

> What, then, is the nature of this fellowship, this unity, both within and between churches? Again we must look at the nature of the Godhead, because it is a picture, not just to be our example, but our very means of bringing this to pass:
>
> > *that all of them may be one, Father, just as you are in me and I am in you... (John 17:21)*
>
> The parallel drawn here is between the unity and fellowship of the Father and the Son, and the unity and fellowship of all true saints.
>
> We are to be one in the same way that the Father and the Son are one; and so we are to enjoy fellowship with each other in the same way that the Godhead has enjoyed fellowship for eternity.
>
> How did Jesus fellowship with His Father in eternity, and be one with Him? The answer is that He lived with Him. He beheld Him. He loved Him. He experienced Him. He knew Him. He enjoyed Him.
>
> There was no denominational structure within the Godhead. There was life. There was no imposed organization – just living fellowship.
>
> And it will be the same within and between churches. What God is going to do, and is even now doing, is to bring to pass living fellowship. He is not going to initiate another pattern of ritual and religious ceremony. He is not going to establish another denomination, another set of formal systems of leadership, another structured religious organization. He is bringing about fellowship.

---

[10] From *In Him Was Life* by Malcolm Webber, pp. 84-88.

This is not one group swallowing up other groups to form some "mega-church." This is fellowship. This is participation in the Divinely-imparted life of one another. This is fellowship. This is fellowship with Jesus in one another. And this is what God is doing in this hour.

God is not building another formal, binding ecclesiastical structure; but He is building, by His Spirit, living organic fellowship. He is building together a fit dwelling-place for Himself (Eph. 2:22).

Christian unity is not a unity of structure, but of fellowship. It is not an outward identification with other Christians or churches or movements. It is a living, spiritual union.

When we speak of "fellowship" in this context, we do not mean superficial relationships, but Divine fellowship. We are not referring to mere friendliness or co-operation, or just doing things together. We mean a living, spiritual fellowship; participating in the life of Jesus in each other; beholding Him in one another; touching Him, and being touched by Him, through each other. It is a fellowship that proceeds spontaneously from the overflowing reality of the indwelling Presence of Jesus Christ in our hearts and lives.

It is through true spiritual fellowship with each other that we are touched by Him; and when His hand touches us, we are changed. This is how the saints minister to each other for the building up of the body of Christ. This is how "the whole body (is) joined and held together by every supporting ligament." This is what happens "as each part does its work." This is how "the whole body grows and builds itself up in love" (Eph. 4:12-16).

This is the process of corporate spiritual maturity. This is Christ dwelling in the hearts of His people, in ever-increasing revelation of Himself. This is all the saints coming to the experiential knowledge of the fullness of His love. This is the church which will soon be "filled to the measure of all the fullness of God" (Eph. 3:17-19).

And it is through fellowship.

Again, by "fellowship" we do not mean shallow friendships, but intimate, spiritual friendships; spiritual communion; the expression of Divine life within God's people.

Christian fellowship is a heart to heart, "deep calls to deep," intimate spiritual communion. It is a profound perception of Jesus Christ in one another; enjoying Jesus in each other. It is a receiving from Him through each other; a giving of Him one to another. It is fellowshipping with Him – together. It is participation in the eternal fellowship of the Godhead – together. It is participation in the everlasting love of the Godhead – together.

Think of the eternal fellowship of the Father, Son and Holy Spirit. Think of the joyful, loving, living, abundant fellowship within the Godhead. That is the life of His church.

Jesus gave us a new commandment:

> *...Love one another. As I have loved you, so you must love one another. (John 13:34)*

Our love to each other is to be "as" Jesus loved us. How could we love one another with Jesus' love, unless He Himself were abiding within us to love? And how could our brother be worthy of such love, except Jesus were abiding in him to receive it?

> *...whatever you did for one of the least of these brothers of mine, you did for me. (Matt. 25:40)*

As we love one another, we love Him. As we enjoy one another, we enjoy Him. In caring for each other, we care for Him. In opening our hearts and lives to one another, we invite His Presence. In serving each other, we kiss His feet. In pouring out our lives for one another, we pour out His love back to Him. As we prefer one another, we give Him the preeminence. As we behold each other, we perceive His beauty. As we embrace one another with self-giving love, we taste His sweetness. As we wash each other's feet, we smell His fragrance.

Jesus dwells in His church – to love and to be loved. As we love one another, quickly and imperceptibly the one love passes over into the other, and we love Him. As we fellowship with each other, quietly and almost unnoticeably we come in contact with Him. And the loving fellowship with which we embrace our brother ascends to that with which we love God, and we are united together in the eternal love and fellowship of the Godhead.

> *...if we love one another, God lives in us and his love is made complete in us. (1 John 4:12)*

Church life is both a foretaste and a beginning of everlasting life. As we love one another, we participate in the eternal love and fellowship of the Godhead, joyfully awaiting the fullness of this union, in the realm which is to come.

In our lonely culture of isolated individualism, God's call to authentic community stands as a warm beacon of light. American culture values and promotes individualism, but God created man for community. We all need nurturing relationships that ground and sustain us. According to a Zulu proverb, "A person is not a person without other people."

Leaders, too, need healthy communities around them – communities that will uphold and strengthen them – communities that are characterized by open communication, candor, loving accountability, trust, and unconditional acceptance – communities that will challenge them to authentic leadership – communities within which they will find personal maturity and fulfillment. In these "safe environments," people have the freedom to be honest and to grow within boundaries framed by shared values and common goals. Such healthy organizational communities nurture character. Although many capacities can be developed outside of intimate, authentic relationships, character cannot. [11]

The Balance of Purposes

Effective spiritual communities achieve a balance between a single, overall community purpose *and* the various purposes of the individuals within the community. This means the community has one broad overarching calling from God to fulfill *and* that this overarching calling embraces and unifies the various callings of those within the community.

We do not want to have just one or the other. We should not have to choose between a single community purpose that every individual is required to mindlessly conform to, at the one extreme, and a multitude of unrelated, individualistic purposes that have no cohesion, structure or meaning together, at the other extreme.

We must have both community purpose and individual purpose. In fact, healthy community forms the context in which individual callings and responsibilities are expressed in order to fulfill the community's corporate purpose.

Consider the following depictions of possible relationships between community purpose and individual purpose:

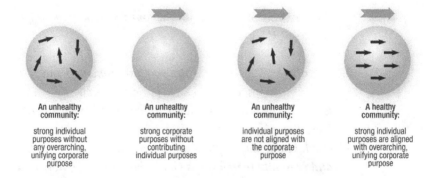

An unhealthy community:	An unhealthy community:	An unhealthy community:	A healthy community:
strong individual purposes without any overarching, unifying corporate purpose	strong corporate purposes without contributing individual purposes	individual purposes are not aligned with the corporate purpose	strong individual purposes are aligned with overarching, unifying corporate purpose

---

[11] Adapted from *The Ascent of a Leader* by Thrall, McNicol & McElrath.

In a healthy community, the individual callings work together to fulfill the community's overarching calling. One flows out of the other:

> *From him the whole body, joined and held together by every supporting ligament, grows and builds itself up in love, as each part does its work. (Eph. 4:16)*

The Twofold Place of Community

Community serves a twofold place in the life of the leader:

1. The healthy leader is *built* in community (Eph. 4:13-16). No healthy leader will ever be developed in a vacuum. The hottest ember grows cold in isolation.

    It is relatively easy to live victoriously when we are all by ourselves. The "spiritual lone ranger" is not tested as deeply as the man who lives in community. It is easy to be patient when no one is irritating us! It is when we come together that we have the opportunity to be patient, kind, forgiving and loving, to walk in servanthood and grace toward one another. As someone said, the Christian life would be easy if it weren't for the devil and people! In reality, we only mature and grow as Christians in the context of community.

    > *As iron sharpens iron, so one man sharpens another. (Prov. 27:17)*

    > *Do not lie to each other, since you have taken off your old self with its practices and have put on the new self, which is being renewed in knowledge in the image of its Creator. Here there is no Greek or Jew, circumcised or uncircumcised, barbarian, Scythian, slave or free, but Christ is all, and is in all. Therefore, as God's chosen people, holy and dearly loved, clothe yourselves with compassion, kindness,*

humility, gentleness and patience. Bear with each other and forgive whatever grievances you may have against one another. Forgive as the Lord forgave you. And over all these virtues put on love, which binds them all together in perfect unity. (Col. 3:9-14)

The leader is built in community. Jesus grew in community, subject to His parents and a part of the community around Him (Luke 2:41-52). Paul was built in community in the school of Gamaliel (Acts 22:3) and then in the church after he was saved (Acts 9:19, 27). According to church tradition, even the apparently individualistic John the Baptist matured in community.

2. The leader *leads* in the context of community (Rom. 12:4-8; 1 Cor. 12:12-27).

    ...in Christ we who are many form one body, and each member belongs to all the others. (Rom. 12:5)

He never grows to the point where he no longer needs vital relationships with others around him. Effective Christian leaders lead in a context of community – not as tough "ministry islands" off by themselves. In the body of Christ, no members are independent (1 Cor. 12).

    The body is a unit, though it is made up of many parts; and though all its parts are many, they form one body. So it is with Christ. (1 Cor. 12:12)

Jesus ministered in community – He was, except for brief times of solitude and prayer, always with the twelve and the other disciples. Jesus had friends and He needed them. Jesus needed their fellowship and support.

    ...My soul is overwhelmed with sorrow to the point of death. Stay here and keep watch with me. (Matt. 26:38)

He was grieved when they fell asleep in the garden (Matt. 26:36-45).

Paul also had friends, and they nurtured and strengthened him:

> *You know that the household of Stephanas were the first converts in Achaia, and they have devoted themselves to the service of the saints. I urge you, brothers, to submit to such as these and to everyone who joins in the work, and labors at it. I was glad when Stephanas, Fortunatus and Achaicus arrived, because they have supplied what was lacking from you. For they refreshed my spirit and yours also... (1 Cor. 16:15-18)*

Significantly, Stephanas was Paul's own convert! Paul was not too proud to receive nurture and support from his own spiritual son. Onesiphorus also was a friend to Paul and strengthened him in "many ways," doubtless including emotionally and spiritually:

> *May the Lord show mercy to the household of Onesiphorus, because he often refreshed me and was not ashamed of my chains. On the contrary, when he was in Rome, he searched hard for me until he found me. May the Lord grant that he will find mercy from the Lord on that day! You know very well in how many ways he helped me in Ephesus. (2 Tim. 1:16-18; cf. 2 Cor. 7:6-7)*

Romans 16:1-16 mentions several of Paul's "dear" friends and even a spiritual "mother" in verse 13![12]

> *Greet Rufus, chosen in the Lord, and his mother, who has been a mother to me, too. (Rom. 16:13)*

---

[12] According to Ken Williams in *A Model for Mutual Care*, Paul's "letters mention at least 75 specific friends and colleagues. These were significant people in his life, many of whom ministered to him."

The following table summarizes Paul's relationships with various communities he was part of:

The Church at Jerusalem	Mutual respect and acceptance. Mutual affirmation. No rivalry. No walls between them. Fellowship in the Word. Sharing of material resources. Paul served them. He brought correction to them. He was willingly accountable to them.
The Church at Antioch	Paul was a committed member of the church. He was accountable to them. He was commissioned by them. He was built by them. He served in the church. He received their prayer support. Perhaps he received their financial support.
Paul's Ministry Team	Partnership together. Sharing of vision and responsibilities. Mutual acceptance and forgiveness. Ministering together. He genuinely nurtured his team. He cared for them (spiritual wellbeing, family, health, daily life). He had deep love and commitment to them.

The Churches Paul Planted	He built them.
	He equipped them.
	He received ministry from them.
	He built emerging leaders.
	He appointed their leadership.
	They were accountable to him.
	He gave them nurture and care.
	He traveled to visit them.
	He wrote to them.
	He was their spiritual father, friend and brother.
	He corrected and affirmed them.
	He had deep travail for them.
	They prayed for him.
	They supported him.

Paul, clearly, had a strong commitment to community!

If Jesus, the Son of God, and Paul, the mighty apostle, needed friends, who are we that we don't? It is not a sign of strength to be by yourself in leadership. It is a mark of weakness. Leaders need friends!

The community is like the soil in which the leader grows – a plant is never independent of the soil!

Thus, community serves a twofold place in the life of the leader:

1. The healthy leader is built in community.
2. The healthy leader leads in community.

These two points do not refer merely to an ideological commitment to "community" but to genuine, committed, nurturing and accountable relationships. As Dietrich Bonhoeffer wrote, "He who loves community destroys community. He who loves the brothers builds community." The author has known people who loudly declared their great love for "New Testament church life"; it was people they were not too fond of!

Four Kinds of Community

The leader needs to be properly connected with four kinds of community: his family, his local church, the various ministry teams of which he is a part, and the world.

- The leader's relationship with his family:

  - His family should be a small spiritual community, providing him with his first-priority spiritual relationships.
  - His family will provide him with experiential "practice" in leadership (1 Tim. 3:4-5).
  - He must have a strong physical and emotional relationship with his spouse so he is protected from temptation.

- The leader's relationship with his local church:

  - In the church, the leader needs to share in the mundane responsibilities of everyday life, and not only "big" leadership responsibilities. The leader needs this opportunity for the development of his own patience, servant-spirit, humility, long-suffering, etc.
  - Like Jesus, the leader must maintain relationships with "normal" people in the church and not only with an elite club of "ministry peers." Many are the leaders who have lost touch with reality by being out of touch with "normal" people. To be healthy, Christian leaders need friends.[13]
  - Accountability. Perhaps King David would not have fallen into sin as he did, if he had lived in genuine accountability within the community.
  - Security and support. The author can testify from his own life about two personal crises he has endured. The first one

---

[13] It is likely that not only spiritual health but also physical health results from friendships. Recent medical research suggests that people who have many quality friends they see on a regular basis are less likely to develop heart disease.

was relatively minor but almost crushed him since he was not part of a strong community at the time. However, he was able to much better endure the second crisis – which was far greater in magnitude – because of the strong spiritual community surrounding him at that time. Too many spiritual leaders report a lack of healthy friendships with others. It is absolutely vital that a leader live and lead with a loving and accepting relational "blanket" around him.

- The leader's relationship with his various ministry teams:

  - The leader is complete when he's part of a team. In the team we have the whole balance of many gifts and strengths – individually we are crippled (Rom. 12:4-5).
  - Every leader needs friendship, encouragement and insight from peers in ministry.
  - In the context of a team, the individual finds true and healthy accountability.

- The leader's relationship with the world:

  - In the eyes of the world, the spiritual leader must have integrity (2 Cor. 4:2; 1 Tim. 3:7).
  - He should treat the lost with respect, care and kindness (Tit. 3:1-2).
  - United with Jesus' heart of compassion for the lost, the Christian leader should be a soul winner, although not necessarily an "evangelist" (Matt. 11:19; 1 Cor. 9:19-23).
  - The leader should willingly and joyfully endure persecution for righteousness' sake, through which he will establish right priorities and be refined and matured (1 Pet. 1:6-7).

It is in community (and not in the vacuum of individualism) that character is formed *and* sustained – genuine Christian character.

chapter 4

Character

No leader will be perfect – other than the Lord Jesus. However, since God's leaders reflect God Himself to men, they must be of the highest character. This was why Moses received such a harsh judgment (Num. 20:7-12). God's work will be done in God's way, in a manner consistent with God's holiness and character.

> The minister's shortcomings simply cannot be concealed. Even the most trivial soon get known.... However trifling their offenses, these little things seem great to others, since everyone measures sin, not by the size of the offense, but by the standing of the sinner. *John Chrysostom (347-407)*

> He who is required by the necessity of his position to speak the highest things is compelled by the same necessity to exemplify the highest things. *Gregory the Great (540-604)*

> Since you [O Lord] have appointed this blind guide to lead them [your people], for their sakes, Lord, if not for mine, teach him whom you have made to be their teacher; lead him whom you have bidden to lead them; rule him who is their ruler. *Aelred (1109-1167)*

> Prayer, meditation, and temptation make a minister. *Martin Luther (1483-1546)*

> Those whom the Lord has destined for this great office he previ-

ously provides with the armor which is requisite for the discharge of it, that they may not come empty and unprepared. *John Calvin (1509-1564)*

I go out to preach with two propositions in mind. First, every person ought to give his life to Christ. Second, whether or not anyone else gives him his life, I will give him mine. *Jonathan Edwards (1703-1758)*

It is the quality of leaders that they can bear to be sat on, absorb shocks, act as a buffer, bear being much plagued. The wear and tear and the continual friction and trials which come to the servants of God are the greatest test of character. *Fred Mitchell, a one-time leader in the old China Inland Mission*

People are not only motivated to follow by the leader's captivating vision or by his compelling communication skills, but also by their sense of the leader's desire to serve, his high integrity and consistency. People will only follow someone they trust, and trust follows character:

We put no stumbling block in anyone's path, so that our ministry will not be discredited. (2 Cor. 6:3)

In everything set them an example by doing what is good. In your teaching show integrity, seriousness and soundness of speech that cannot be condemned, so that those who oppose you may be ashamed because they have nothing bad to say about us. (Tit. 2:7-8)

Character is not a "recommended optional extra" for a leader; it is a "non-negotiable" requirement.

Sadly, today, due to a lack of integrity in many leaders, organizational trust has declined. According to one 2006 study in the corporate world, only 51% of employees have trust and confidence in senior management, only 36% of employees believe their leaders act with honesty and integrity, and over the past 12 months, 76% of employees have observed illegal or unethical conduct on the job – conduct which, if exposed, would seriously violate the public trust. This lack of trust undermines organizational effectiveness.

Such problems are not limited to the business world. One man had a powerful calling from God to be an evangelist. He had a compelling vision to reach his nation, and with great signs and wonders accompanying, he led many people to the Lord and established a movement ultimately consisting of hundreds of churches. Then it was revealed that for years he had lived in a series of adulterous relationships, and his followers were devastated. The movement he established continues to this day under different leadership, but it has never regained its former glory. This man had an extraordinary calling as well as strong abilities to lead and build an organization but he lacked integrity and accountability.

> *The man of integrity walks securely, but he who takes crooked paths will be found out. (Prov. 10:9)*

> *Not everyone who says to me, "Lord, Lord," will enter the kingdom of heaven, but only he who does the will of my Father who is in heaven. Many will say to me on that day, "Lord, Lord, did we not prophesy in your name, and in your name drive out demons and perform many miracles?" Then I will tell them plainly, "I never knew you. Away from me, you evildoers!" (Matt. 7:21-23)*

King Saul had great abilities and a genuine calling, but he lacked integrity, so his leadership failed in the end. Ultimately, God is more interested in who we are than in what we do. Thus, we should be strong in both gifts and fruit.

> *But you, man of God, flee from all this, and pursue righteousness, godliness, faith, love, endurance and gentleness. (1 Tim. 6:11)*

> *… set an example for the believers in speech, in life, in love, in faith and in purity. Until I come, devote yourself to the public reading*

of Scripture, to preaching and to teaching. Do not neglect your gift, which was given you through a prophetic message when the body of elders laid their hands on you.Be diligent in these matters; give yourself wholly to them, so that everyone may see your progress. Watch your life and doctrine closely. Persevere in them, because if you do, you will save both yourself and your hearers. (1 Tim. 4:12-16)

Similarly, one may have received some excellent training that has produced sound competencies in one's life, but without character, the leader will eventually fail.

Training Fails When Character Is Not Developed[14]

Here at the edge of the Ozarks where we live, many young workers are sent by home mission boards to help the unchurched and under-privileged. Because this work is often hard, demanding and unrewarding many fail. Most often the reason for their failure is simply a lack of character development – not a lack of formal scholastic training.

Scholastic accomplishment neither makes nor breaks a missionary. It is but one factor in the complex of influences which have formed the man himself. A man may be highly trained in medicine, in linguistics or in Bible knowledge, yet be an utter failure in his assigned task. Why? Because his training was deficient? Not at all, if you are speaking in a formal sense of skills acquired. It is the human factor, any mission director will tell you, that crumbles. Hands skilled to operate on sick bodies, tongue quick to frame strange sounds, mind stored with hundreds of Bible verses – all this can be true, but the man himself may still be untrained – lacking in character development.

Formal training can be a most subtle stumbling block to its

---

[14] Quoted from *No Other Foundation* by DeVern Fromke.

own usefulness. In our human way of thinking, formal training carries with it some sort of prestige that feeds personal pride, so that in the field of his specialization a man is afraid to make a mistake lest he appear incompetent. The application of hard-earned skills and knowledge to new situations where mistakes in action and judgment may become obvious to others demands genuine humility and moral courage.

Often those with the highest grades in language courses, for example, when faced with another language where that particular skill will no longer serve, find that fear and pride paralyze their efforts. Such failure is not due to lack of ability or skill, but to the character of the individual. He has in fact failed to learn from and during his training the very thing that alone can now make it useful in application.

Essential training, then, should produce disciplined – self-disciplined, Spirit-disciplined men – who know how to exercise wise control over their time, appetites, passions, tongue, thoughts; men who have learned how to operate on a Spirit-directed system of priorities, on their own, away from the helpful stimulus of Christian fellowship and meetings, or in the midst of pressure toward mediocrity among many Christians. We can see why so much training has failed; it is not mere skills and knowledge attained but the *character produced* that is basic to the resilience and flexibility necessary to meet situations without cracking.

There are several lists in the New Testament of the specific character qualities of a godly leader:

> *...love, joy, peace, patience, kindness, goodness, faithfulness, gentleness and self-control... (Gal. 5:22-23)*

> *...make every effort to add to your faith goodness; and to goodness, knowledge; and to knowledge, self-control; and to self-control, perse-*

verance; and to perseverance, godliness; and to godliness, brotherly kindness; and to brotherly kindness, love. For if you possess these qualities in increasing measure, they will keep you from being ineffective and unproductive in your knowledge of our Lord Jesus Christ. (2 Pet. 1:5-8)

Please read 1 Timothy 3 and Titus 1 for extensive lists of the character qualities necessary in a godly leader.

How Is Character Formed?[15]

As we have seen, the ultimate purpose of Christian leaders is to know God[16]:

this is eternal life: that they may know you, the only true God, and Jesus Christ, whom you have sent. (John 17:3)

Jesus has called us to walk with Him, to love Him, to fellowship with Him; and as we fellowship inwardly with Jesus, we experience transformation in our lives:

But whenever anyone turns to the Lord, the veil is taken away. Now the Lord is the Spirit, and where the Spirit of the Lord is, there is freedom. And we, who with unveiled faces all contemplate the Lord's glory, are being transformed into his likeness with ever-increasing glory, which comes from the Lord, who is the Spirit. (2 Cor. 3:16-18, Greek)

As we look at God, He daily transforms us into the image of Jesus by the Holy Spirit. *This* is the formation of character in the leader's life.

---

[15] The following is adapted from the booklet, *The Transforming Work of the Holy Spirit in the Christian's Life* by Malcolm Webber.

[16] This is covered in detail in *To Enjoy Him Forever* by Malcolm Webber.

Character formation is not a matter of *our own* goodness shining forth.

> *...all our righteous acts are like filthy rags... (Is. 64:6)*

> *Abide in me, and I will abide in you. No branch can bear fruit by itself; it must abide in the vine. Neither can you bear fruit unless you abide in me. (John 15:4)*

Christian character is not the result of us gritting our teeth and trying to do "the right thing" or "what Jesus would do"; it is *the formation of the image of Christ* in our lives and ministries that constitutes true character development.[17]

But how does God actually do this work of transformation in our lives and how can we best respond to it?

Here is a simple model of the three ways the Holy Spirit works in our lives to build character. Here is the model:

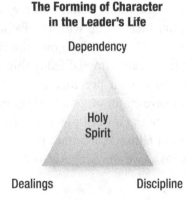

**The Forming of Character
in the Leader's Life**

Dependency

Holy
Spirit

Dealings   Discipline

According to this model, Christian character formation is the result of three kinds of work of the Holy Spirit. These are the three paths to transformation:

---

[17] Character is not "first"; Christ is first and from Him everything else comes!

- Divine Dependence
- Dramatic Dealings
- Daily Discipline

These three kinds of work are all motivated by the Holy Spirit and they are used by Him to transform our lives and ministries into the image of Christ.

As we will see, all three of these works can have dangers associated with them, if we are unbalanced and emphasize one over the others. We need all three.

We will also see that we can intentionally respond in ways that will facilitate or "develop" all three of these works in our lives.

The Three Works of the Holy Spirit

1. DEPENDENCY

Dependency refers to a continuous walking in the Spirit. Just as Jesus lived in continuous inward fellowship with His Father, so we are to be continuously dependent on God. As we do this, the Holy Spirit changes us. This means living in constant inward fellowship with God – living minute by minute in the inward presence of the Lord Jesus by His Spirit. This does not involve emotions and feelings necessarily, but it is a spiritual consciousness of the inward presence of God. It is a lifestyle of inwardly drawing from Him life, wisdom, peace and strength. It is a total dependence on God as we continuously look at Him with the eyes of our hearts.

Jesus gave us a wonderful promise of abiding fellowship with God:

> *... He who loves me will be loved by my Father, and I too will love him and show myself to him...My Father will love him, and we will come to him and make our home with him. (John 14:21-23)*

This is a promise of the manifest ("show myself") and continuous ("our home") presence of God in our hearts. We can live in continuous inward fellowship with Jesus by His Spirit. As we do this, we will have His strength and wisdom to fulfill His purposes:

> *Abide in me, and I will abide in you. No branch can bear fruit by itself; it must abide in the vine. Neither can you bear fruit unless you abide in me. I am the vine; you are the branches. If a man abides in me and I in him, he will bear much fruit; apart from me you can do nothing. (John 15:4-5)*

2. DEALINGS

This refers to the "crisis" events that God allows in our lives. As we properly respond to His dealings in our lives, the Holy Spirit changes us. God's dealings can be both positive and negative.[18] Positive events are when He comes to us and shows us His love and His presence. He can do this both individually and corporately.

Individually, God often comes to His children in special ways and touches us with His love and His presence. It may be while we are in prayer or worship, or it can happen during the normal activities of life. God simply comes and touches us in dramatic ways by His Spirit.

In my early experience as a Christian, I needed a great deal of deliverance from demonic oppression in my life. I received much of this deliverance simply in the presence of God. Without anyone even praying for me, God came to me on a number of occasions as I was praying and He touched me powerfully with His presence and love. In such a condition, my heart was fully open before Him, fully repentant of the former sins that had allowed the enemy access to my life. During these times of the

---

[18] All of God's dealings in our lives are ultimately positive, accomplishing both God's glory and our advancement in His purposes. However, God uses experiences that are both positive and negative to do this. In that sense, we speak here of the dealings of God as being both "positive" and "negative."

manifest presence of God, the demons left – they could not stay in the presence of the Lord!

These positive experiences also happen to us in our corporate meetings. Many times as we worship God He comes with His powerful presence and sets His people free, touching us with His love. It might be a spiritual touch or a mental, emotional or physical touch by His Spirit. Whatever form it takes, it is wonderful!

These are all "positive" events. However, God also allows His people to experience "negative" crisis events through various kinds of temptations, trials, chastisements, sufferings and persecutions.

> *... now for a little while you may have had to suffer grief in all kinds of trials. These have come so that your faith – of greater worth than gold, which perishes even though refined by fire – may be proved genuine and may result in praise, glory and honor when Jesus Christ is revealed. (1 Pet. 1:6-7)*

Peter speaks of "all kinds of trials." This means a diversity of trials – many different *kinds* of trials – not just a great number. God uses many different kinds of difficult experiences and sufferings in His transformational process.

These trials are tests of character. A trial is a test to see if something can stand up to strain. Before you trust the strength of a rope to hold you, you will first give it a trial – you will test it to see if it is strong enough to do what you want.

God allows His emerging leaders to go through different kinds of trials. In persecution, for example, the devil entices leaders to give up their calling, or even their faith, for fear of suffering ridicule, financial loss or physical harm. A temptation to sin is a trial to see if we will choose holiness over sin. Suffering is a trial to see if we will serve God even when things go wrong (e.g., Job). False doctrine is also a test: it may offer us pride and thoughts of elitism, or perhaps an easier way of life. Praise can even be a test (Prov. 27:21). There are many different kinds of trials that God allows in our lives. He is preparing us to reign with Him for eternity (Rev. 2:26; 3:21) and He wants our characters to be strong.

> *No discipline seems pleasant at the time, but painful. Later on, however, it produces a harvest of righteousness and peace for those who have been trained by it. (Heb. 12:11; cf. vv. 6-12)*

> *Now if we are children, then we are heirs – heirs of God and co-heirs with Christ, if indeed we share in his sufferings in order that we may also share in his glory. (Rom. 8:17)*

In 1 Peter 1, Peter also says, "you may have had to suffer." Thus, suffering only takes place because it is necessary – we "have to" suffer. Suffering is necessary for the building of character, for growth to maturity, for transformation into Christ's image.

> *…we also rejoice in our sufferings, because we know that suffering produces perseverance; perseverance, character; and character, hope. (Rom. 5:3)*

Then Peter compares the trials of our faith with the purifying of gold. True faith is tested by trials just as gold (far inferior to faith) is proved by fire. Gold is a precious metal but it can be mixed with impurities that lower its value and spoil its beauty. So it needs to be refined. In the intense heat of fire in a crucible, the impurities rise to the surface of the melted gold and are skimmed off by the goldsmith. The heavenly Goldsmith heats the gold (our lives), brings the impurities to the surface and takes them away; and He does this repeatedly – until when He looks into the gold He sees impurities no longer but only His own image.

If gold that perishes must be tried by fire, how much more does our faith, which is being proved for eternity, need to be tried and purified by fire? God is preparing us for eternity.

Many will be purified, made spotless and refined... those who are wise will understand. (Dan. 12:10)

Do not be afraid of what you are about to suffer. I tell you, the devil will put some of you in prison to test you, and you will suffer persecution for ten days. Be faithful, even to the point of death, and I will give you the crown of life. (Rev. 2:10)

We should not be afraid of these sufferings because God sovereignly oversees all our trials for His own glory and for our perfection.

No temptation has seized you except what is common to man. And God is faithful; he will not let you be tempted beyond what you can bear. But when you are tempted, he will also provide a way out so that you can stand up under it. (1 Cor. 10:13)

The sufferings come in the purpose of God. They are not random or arbitrary. God does not roll a dice or spin a wheel. Satan is not in control; God is, and there are no mistakes with Him. What He allows is always consistent with His infinite wisdom and eternal purpose.

Moreover, as Peter says, God's purpose is that our faith "may be proved genuine" in the judgment of the Last Day. God's purpose is to prove our faith as *genuine*. His intention is not to disprove our faith, or defeat us. Furthermore, in the end, the believer will experience "praise, glory and honor" (cf. 1 Cor. 4:5).

For our light and momentary troubles are achieving for us an eternal glory that far outweighs them all. (2 Cor. 4:17)

And when the Chief Shepherd appears, you will receive the crown of glory that will never fade away. (1 Pet. 5:4)

Because this is the glorious purpose of trials, we can rejoice in the midst of our tests.

Dear friends, do not be surprised at the painful trial you are suffering, as though something strange were happening to you. But rejoice that you participate in the sufferings of Christ, so that you may be overjoyed when his glory is revealed. If you are insulted because of the name of Christ, you are blessed, for the Spirit of glory and of God rests on you. (1 Pet. 4:12-14)

We should rejoice in our times of trial. We should not complain and feel sorry for ourselves. God has given us the privilege of "participating in the sufferings of Christ." Like His, our suffering is undeserved, and it is for His name (cf. Rom. 8:17; 2 Cor. 4:10; Phil. 3:10; Col. 1:24; Heb. 13:13). Moreover, Peter says that our glory with its resultant joy is not only in the age to come but when we suffer for Him "the Spirit of glory and of God" rests upon us now! We can, even now, know a little of the coming glory with its exultant joy.

Thus, there are both "positive" and "negative" kinds of dealings of the Holy Spirit in our lives. If we respond to them the right way, the dealings of God give us opportunities to make "significant leaps" in our relationship with God. But the dealings of God are also dangerous. They can harden us – if we respond wrongly. If we resist the positive dealings of the Holy Spirit and refuse to yield to Him when He comes, or if we respond with bitterness, anger, unforgiveness or offense to the negative dealings of God in our lives, we will grow harder against Him.

He who falls on this stone will be broken to pieces, but he on whom it falls will be crushed. (Matt. 21:44)

If we fall on the Lord Jesus with submission during the dealings of God we will find brokenness and grace. But if we resist God we will be "crushed."

3. DISCIPLINE

There are several vital disciplines in the life of the emerging leader.

First, there are our daily disciplined times with God. The Holy Spirit changes us as we come before Him regularly. We all need disciplined daily devotional lives – times that we "devote" to God, coming apart from every other activity.

Moreover, we need to seek God as a daily discipline, whether we feel like it or not, whether we think that we sense the presence of God or not. This devotional discipline includes prayer, meditation, quietness before God, systematic personal study of the Word of God, sitting under teaching, fasting, group praise and worship, giving, family devotional times and so forth.

Second, there is the discipline of the heart.

> Do you not know that in a race all the runners run, but only one gets the prize? Run in such a way as to get the prize. Everyone who competes in the games goes into strict training. They do it to get a crown that will not last; but we do it to get a crown that will last forever. Therefore I do not run like a man running aimlessly; I do not fight like a man beating the air. No, I beat my body and make it my slave so that after I have preached to others, I myself will not be disqualified for the prize. (1 Cor. 9:24-27)

> Whoever has no rule over his own spirit Is like a city broken down, without walls. (Prov. 25:28)

Without the essential quality of discipline, all other leadership virtues remain stunted; they cannot grow. J. Oswald Sanders wrote[19]:

Before we can conquer the world, we must first conquer the self.

---

[19] *Spiritual Leadership*, p. 52.

A leader is a person who has learned to obey a discipline imposed from without, and has then taken on a more rigorous discipline from within. Those who rebel against authority, and scorn self-discipline – who shirk the rigors and turn from the sacrifices – do not qualify to lead. Many who drop out of ministry are sufficiently gifted, but have large areas of life floating free from the Holy Spirit's control. Lazy and disorganized people never rise to true leadership.

Thus, the progression of discipline in the life of a leader is as follows: First, he submits to discipline *from without*. By doing so, he develops discipline *from within*. When that is mature, he is then permitted by God *to give* discipline to others. He has become a leader.

> *Paul, an apostle of Christ Jesus by the command of God our Savior and of Christ Jesus our hope, (1 Tim. 1:1)*

Paul's choice of the word "command" is significant. In this letter he commands Timothy to command the church and the false teachers to do certain things. Thus, he who gives commands is himself under command (cf. Prov. 10:8). Paul was not only under God's command; he was also accountable to the church at Antioch (Acts 13:3; 14:26-28; 15:2-3, 35-40; 18:22-23) as well as to the leaders in Jerusalem (Acts 21:17-26; Gal. 2:2).

True character is formed in the context of Christ and Community in these three stages:

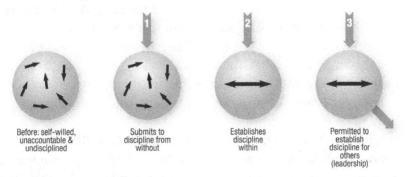

| Before: self-willed, unaccountable & undisciplined | Submits to discipline from without | Establishes discipline within | Permitted to establish dsicipline for others (leadership) |

1. First, the emerging leader submits to discipline. He trusts God and others. In this initial stage, the leader humbly commits himself to God and to those around him. He chooses to trust others with the deepest parts of his life. He becomes vulnerable, coming under another's influence and submitting himself to others' strengths.

2. Then, in that context, internal discipline is built. This is self-discipline, self-control (1 Cor. 9:25-27). Thus, the emerging leader aligns himself with the truth. As he listens to those around him, their advice and correction (in line with the Word of God) will nurture his character. As he submits himself to someone outside of himself – instead of simply following his own direction as he had always done previously – he builds internal discipline. He finds internal reality. He is challenged and he pays the price. As the leader grows in responsibilities, his commitment to integrity will inevitably be tested. The nurturing community strengthens him to choose the right way – whatever it may cost him. This is how character is developed.

3. Once internal discipline is in place, God permits him – and man trusts him – to lead others. Thus, he discovers his destiny. This is where the leader – strong in both capacity and character – truly fulfills his Divine purpose.

This order cannot be reversed and none of the steps can be skipped. Internal discipline must be in place in the leader before he can effectively lead others, and his own external discipline must be in place before he can build true inward discipline. Thus, if one does not truly submit himself to another (stage 1), he should never be trusted with true leadership responsibility (stage 3); he has not yet begun to build true character.

Furthermore, it is extremely important to understand that these three stages are *cumulative*. They are not sequential in the sense of abandoning one when moving to the next. They do not replace each other. The healthy leader *maintains* both his submission to others and his internal self-discipline while he leads others.

The following graphic shows another way of presenting these three stages using slightly different terms: the emerging leader submits to leadership, thus establishes self-leadership, and is consequently given the right to exercise leadership.

In order to be able to assume the responsibility for other people's growth, leaders must themselves have grown to true maturity and inner freedom. They must not be locked up in a prison of illusion or selfishness, and they must have allowed others to guide them.

We can only command if we know how to obey. We can only be a leader if we know how to be a servant. We can only be a mother- or a father-figure if we are conscious of ourselves as a daughter or a son. Jesus is the Lamb before the He is the Shepherd. His authority comes from the Father; He is the beloved Son of the Father.[20]

We Need All Three Works of the Holy Spirit

These three works are quite different in nature:

- Dependency is a continuous process: moment by moment we draw near to God; the other two are more "intermittent" in nature.[21]

- The dealings of God produce significant leaps of growth in our lives; the other two works involve steady advancement.

---

[20] *Community and Growth* by Jean Vanier, p. 225.

[21] Of course, the spiritual disciplines should be regular occurrences in our lives.

- Discipline brings us objectivity; the other two works are more subjective.

We need all three of these works of the Spirit in our lives. Each of the three strengthens and is strengthened by the others.

When we live in continuous inward dependency on God, our devotional times will be much richer and more effective, our inward discipline of heart will be more focused, and we will be more able to respond properly to both the positive and negative dealings of God in our lives (Rom. 8:35-39).

When we allow the Holy Spirit to change us through the crisis events that He allows, that will greatly increase our inward fellowship with Him and it will also enhance our devotional and inward disciplines.

When we discipline our lives to seek God daily and to submit to His purposes whether we feel like it or not, that builds a context in which it will be easier to respond appropriately to His dealings when they come, and it also strengthens our continuous dependency on God.

When we have all three in our lives there is balance and strength.

The Three Paths in the Life of Jesus

We see all three of these paths in Jesus' life.

1. DEPENDENCY

As we saw in Chapter 2, during His earthly ministry, Jesus lived in continuous fellowship with His Father, and through that fellowship He drew from, and lived by, His Father's life. It was through His fellowship with His Father.

2. DEALINGS

Jesus experienced great crisis events in His life and ministry – both positive and negative.

"Positive" events included His water baptism, His experience on the Mount of Transfiguration, and His resurrection.

"Negative" crisis events included Jesus' temptations by Satan, His betrayal by Judas, His agony in the Garden of Gethsemane, His rejection by men, and His death on the cross.

3. DISCIPLINE

Jesus was disciplined in the Word of God. Even as a Child of twelve, He knew the Word of God very well (Luke 2:46-47).

Jesus was disciplined in prayer:

> *Very early in the morning, while it was still dark, Jesus got up, left the house and went off to a solitary place, where he prayed. (Mark 1:35)*

> *After he had dismissed them, he went up on a mountainside by himself to pray. When evening came, he was there alone, (Matt. 14:23)*

Occasionally, Jesus spent entire nights in communion with His Father:

> *One of those days Jesus went out to a mountainside to pray, and spent the night praying to God. (Luke 6:12)*

He not only prayed alone but also in the company of His disciples:

> *One day Jesus was praying in a certain place. When he finished, one of his disciples said to him, "Lord, teach us to pray, just as John taught his disciples." (Luke 11:1)*

Jesus prayed so well that after one of these times of prayer before His disciples, they were so conscious of their own comparative inadequacy in prayer that they requested, "Lord, teach us to pray."

He was also disciplined in fasting (Luke 4:2), and in corporate worship:

> He went to Nazareth, where he had been brought up, and on the Sabbath day he went into the synagogue, as was his custom... (Luke 4:16).

Jesus also came under the discipline of the human community around Him:

> Then he went down to Nazareth with them and was obedient to them [his parents]... (Luke 2:51)

Of course, He was always submitted to the discipline of His Father:

> Although he was a son, he learned obedience from what he suffered (Heb. 5:8)

Thus, Jesus lived on all three paths; we need to as well.

The Three Paths in the Life of Paul

Paul, the apostle, is a tremendous example of a leader who walked on these three paths.

1. DEPENDENCY

Paul lived in continuous fellowship with God by His Spirit. That fellowship was the source of all character and fruitfulness in his life and ministry:

> I can do everything through him who gives me strength. (Phil. 4:13)

... in all these things we are more than conquerors through him who loved us. (Rom. 8:37)

I have been crucified with Christ and I no longer live, but Christ lives in me. The life I live in the body, I live by faith in the Son of God, who loved me and gave himself for me. (Gal. 2:20)

But by the grace of God I am what I am, and his grace to me was not without effect. No, I worked harder than all of them – yet not I, but the grace of God that was with me. (1 Cor. 15:10)

Moreover, this was the lifestyle that Paul taught others:

being strengthened with all power according to his glorious might so that you may have great endurance and patience, and joyfully giving thanks to the Father... (Col. 1:11-12)

So then, just as you received Christ Jesus as Lord, continue to live in him, rooted and built up in him, strengthened in the faith as you were taught, and overflowing with thankfulness. (Col. 2:6-7)

2. DEALINGS

Paul was no stranger to the dealings of God. He regularly experienced "positive crises":

... I will go on to visions and revelations from the Lord. I know a man in Christ who fourteen years ago was caught up to the third heaven. Whether it was in the body or out of the body I do not know – God knows. And I know that this man – whether in the body or apart from the body I do not know, but God knows – was caught up to paradise. He heard inexpressible things, things that man is not permitted to tell. (2 Cor. 12:1-4)

Of course, it was not all positive for Paul. He, perhaps more often, also experienced the "negative" dealings of God for his transformation:

To keep me from becoming conceited because of these surpass-ingly great revelations, there was given me a thorn in my flesh, a messenger of Satan, to torment me. Three times I pleaded with the Lord to take it away from me. But he said to me, "My grace is sufficient for you, for my power is made perfect in weakness." Therefore I will boast all the more gladly about my weaknesses, so that Christ's power may rest on me. That is why, for Christ's sake, I delight in weaknesses, in insults, in hardships, in persecu-tions, in difficulties. For when I am weak, then I am strong. (2 Cor. 12:7-10)

But we have this treasure in jars of clay to show that this all-surpassing power is from God and not from us. We are hard pressed on every side, but not crushed; perplexed, but not in despair; persecuted, but not abandoned; struck down, but not destroyed. We always carry around in our body the death of Jesus, so that the life of Jesus may also be revealed in our body. For we who are alive are always being given over to death for Jesus' sake, so that his life may be revealed in our mortal body. (2 Cor. 4:7-11)

3. DISCIPLINE

Paul also was a disciplined man. He did not allow himself to become self-indulgent, complacent or lethargic.

... I beat my body and make it my slave so that after I have preached to others, I myself will not be disqualified for the prize. (1 Cor. 9:27)

Finally, as we will see later in this chapter under "Accountability," Paul was also submitted in his heart to the discipline of the church community around him.

Other Biblical Examples of All Three Paths

Here are some biblical examples of various people of God who walked on these three paths.

1. DEPENDENCY

John, the "disciple whom Jesus loved," lived in the abiding presence of God. Many decades after Jesus' ascension, John wrote that "our fellowship is with the Father, and with his Son Jesus Christ" (1 John 1:3). John did not say that his fellowship "was" with God but that it "is" with God.

John lived in continuous inward fellowship with God by the Holy Spirit. Out of that inward life John lived and ministered. The result was some of the greatest writings in the entire Bible about the Person of Jesus Christ as God, as well as the nature of the Christian life as union with God.

2. DEALINGS

Jacob had a profound encounter with God in Genesis 32. His wrestling with God resulted in a significant leap of growth in his character; his permanent physical limp no doubt outwardly represented his deep inward brokenness as a direct result of the dealings of God.

King David sinned against God on several occasions and through the very negative dealings of God came to a higher place in his life. For example, Psalm 51 details the depth of his brokenness and submission to God after his chastisement for the sin with Bathsheba.

3. DISCIPLINE

Zechariah, the priest, provides us with an excellent example of the fruit of discipline in Luke 1:

Once when Zechariah's division was on duty and he was serving as priest before God, he was chosen by lot, according to the custom of the priesthood, to go into the temple of the Lord and burn incense. And when the time for the burning of incense came, all the assembled worshipers were praying outside. (Luke 1:8-10)

Zechariah was diligently performing his duty, when suddenly he had an extraordinary experience:

Then an angel of the Lord appeared to him, standing at the right side of the altar of incense. (Luke 1:11)

The angel appeared to announce the birth of John the Baptist, the greatest prophet who had ever lived (Luke 7:28)!

Notably, this experience occurred in the context of the fulfilling of duty. What might have happened if Zechariah had "slept in" that day, or if he had not "felt anointed" and so neglected to go to the temple and burn incense as he knew he should have done?

The Perils of Imbalance

All three kinds of work have potential dangers associated with them. If we are not balanced and emphasize one over the others we will get into spiritual trouble. We need all three to be in balance.

- Catholics or other contemplative mystics can have excess in their lives in the area of dependency.

- Many Pentecostals and Charismatics are imbalanced in the area of the "positive" dealings of God, while severely persecuted believers in certain countries can become imbalanced in the area of God's "negative" dealings.

- Evangelicals are sometimes imbalanced in the area of discipline.

The following modification to our model shows the specific dangers of imbalance in each of the three areas.

Imbalances in the Leader's Life

Licentiousness

Imbalance

Lethargy   Legalism

1. IMBALANCE REGARDING DEPENDENCY

One who is always looking inward, but lacks the restraint of a disciplined walk in God as well as the corrective and purging influence of the dealings of God, will sometimes fall into licentiousness. He will end up being led more by his emotions and feelings than by the Holy Spirit.

2. IMBALANCE REGARDING DEALINGS

A person who is imbalanced in his emphasis on the positive dealings of God will frequently fall into spiritual lethargy. Having lost the work of discipline in his life as well as the initiative of continually seeking God minute by minute, such a person will lose a proper sense of initiative. He will jump from experience to experience, no longer taking appropriate daily responsibility for his life.

Furthermore, such people are constantly running around looking for "the next move of God." Their lives are spiritual "roller-coasters"; they are led by their emotions and feelings more than by the purpose of God. Frequently, they worry that God has "left" them because the feelings are not as strong as they once were. They fret about what they must have done to offend God and try to find some place where He is moving in order to "recapture" His presence and favor. They are blissfully unaware that God wants them to actually do something about their spiritual condition and to learn and mature.

There are also those who become imbalanced regarding the "negative" dealings of God. By focusing too much on their sufferings, they can also fall into spiritual lethargy except in a little different manner – they become self-absorbed, infected with self-pity, introverted and negative towards God and the Christian life. Passivity soon replaces responsibility in their lives as they consign themselves to their apparent lot of defeat.

3. IMBALANCE REGARDING DISCIPLINE

The imbalance in the area of discipline is legalism. The Christian who does not enjoy the blessing of the positive dealings of God and the vitality of continuous dependence on the Holy Spirit, often will soon start trusting in himself and his own works to stay right with God and to fulfill His will. Such a leader will not be moving under God's breath as he should be. He will not know God or His grace as he should. Having lost the power of the dramatic dealings of God in his life and the vitality of a continuous walk in God, his life will be largely fruitless – outwardly righteous but inwardly sterile and barren.

We need all three of these works of the Holy Spirit in our lives. In fact, we *must* have all three if we are to mature properly in Christ. God does not tell us to pick and choose between them. Moreover, when we seek to walk in all three paths we will avoid the dangers. Walking in all three provides balance and strength.

Consequently, being strong in one area is good but it is not good enough. We must not rest on our laurels in one area, but work on the others.

Facilitating the Work of the Holy Spirit

The emerging leader is wise to respond positively to these works of the Holy Spirit and thereby facilitate His transformation.

Here is how we can best respond to each kind of work:

1. DEPENDENCY

We can develop this by learning the inner discipline of yielding to the Holy Spirit. This is the "practice of the presence of God." We learn to look inside continuously, finding Him, looking at His face, loving Him inwardly, being loved by Him, talking to Him, listening to His voice. The best book written on this subject is *The Practice of the Presence of God* by Brother Lawrence.

2. DEALINGS

We can facilitate the transforming work of the Holy Spirit through positive dealings by putting ourselves in the place where God is moving. We should get together with one another and seek His face, asking Him to come.

Come near to God and he will come near to you... (Jam. 4:8)

Then, when He comes, we must respond to Him. Sometimes people say they want God to touch them and then when He manifests Himself they hold back and refuse to yield to Him. When God comes, we must yield to Him and let Him have His way in our hearts and lives.

Regarding God's "negative" dealings such as persecution, suffering, trials, and the tragedies of life – we should seek God when they happen and hold as tightly to Him as we can. This is usually hard to do. It is often easier for us to run from God during hard times. But we must seek the Holy Spirit during the difficult, hard times in the midst of tribulation and trial. Then He will use those times in a very positive way to mature us.

3. DISCIPLINE

We must work on developing the daily devotional disciplines. Even the strongest saints need to work on this constantly. The enemy is very good at giving us a thousand reasons why "I don't have time today!"

First, we must establish patterns – appropriate routines. Then we must maintain these disciplines. As already noted, these devotional disciplines include prayer, meditation, quietness before God, systematic personal study of the Word of God, sitting under teaching, fasting, group praise and worship, and so forth.

In addition, we must joyfully embrace the disciplines of heart, submitting ourselves to those God has put around us.

This, then, is our model:

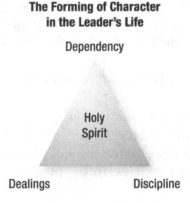

The Forming of Character in the Leader's Life

Dependency

Holy Spirit

Dealings   Discipline

Christian character is formed by the Holy Spirit along these three paths of transformation:

- Divine Dependence
- Dramatic Dealings
- Daily Discipline

These three kinds of work are all motivated by the Holy Spirit and they are used by Him to transform our lives into the mature image of Jesus Christ.

If spiritual transformation were the result of some kind of human ability, then it could only be experienced by the few leaders with that particular ability. However, it is not the result of our wisdom, strength or wealth.

> *This is what the Lord says: "Let not the wise man boast of his wisdom or the strong man boast of his strength or the rich man boast of his riches, but let him who boasts boast about this: that he understands and knows me, that I am the Lord, who exercises kindness, justice and righteousness on earth, for in these I delight," declares the Lord. (Jer. 9:23-24)*

The three paths to transformation have nothing to do with human wealth, education, intelligence, physical strength, physical beauty, family, occupation, social status, religious status, or even the events of our lives in the past.

- Wealth does not count because God owns all things anyway. He is not impressed by anyone's prosperity!
- Education and intelligence do not count because the three paths of transformation are all so simple!
- Strength and beauty do not count because the leader is "in Christ" and not in the flesh.
- Family connections do not count because we have a new family in Christ – the family of God.
- Occupations do not count since God has called all of us to work, ultimately, for Him (1 Cor. 7:21-22; Col. 3:23-24).
- Social and religious status do not count because those things are not impressive to God.
- Even the events of our lives in the past do not count because we are "new creations" in Christ (2 Cor. 5:17)!

These three paths of transformation are not functions of human ability. They are all the work of God's grace in our lives.

Brothers, think of what you were when you were called. Not many of you were wise by human standards; not many were influential; not many were of noble birth. But God chose the foolish things of the world to shame the wise; God chose the weak things of the world to shame the strong. He chose the lowly things of this world and the despised things – and the things that are not – to nullify the things that are, so that no one may boast before him. (1 Cor. 1:26-31)

If we walk on these three paths, God will transform our lives by the power of the Holy Spirit and we will be changed into Jesus' image.

But we all, looking on the glory of the Lord, with unveiled face, are transformed according to the same image from glory to glory, even as by the Lord the Spirit. (2 Cor. 3:18, Darby's translation)

Naturally, this process takes time.

Proving

A leader does not become one overnight. He must be tested first.

They must first be tested; and then if there is nothing against them, let them serve... (1 Tim. 3:10)

He must undergo the preparations of God, which both break and strengthen. Moreover, the more he wants to be used by God as a leader, the more he must submit to the deeper dealings of God in his life.

This goes against our culture, which wants instant success. We want to start at "the top," but that is not the way of God.

The following story[22] is an excellent illustration of the preparation process of God.

---

[22] *The Harness of the Lord* by Bill Britton.

I Saw the King's Carriage

On a dirt road in the middle of a wide field stood a beautiful carriage, something on the order of a stagecoach but all edged in gold and with beautiful carvings. It was pulled by six large chestnut horses: two in the lead, two in the middle and two in the rear. But they were not moving, they were not pulling the carriage, and I wondered why. Then I saw the driver underneath the carriage on the ground on his back just behind the last two horses' heels working on something between the front wheels on the carriage. I thought, *"My, he is in a dangerous place; for if one of those horses kicked or stepped back, they could kill him, or if they decided to go forward, or got frightened somehow, they would pull the carriage right over him."* But he didn't seem afraid for he knew that those horses were disciplined and would not move till he told them to move. The horses were not stamping their feet nor acting restless, and though there were bells on their feet, the bells were not tinkling. There were pom-poms on their harness over their heads but the pom-poms were not moving. They were simply standing still and quiet waiting for the voice of the Master.

There Were Two Young Colts in the Field

As I watched the harnessed horses I noticed two young colts coming out of the open field and they approached the carriage and seemed to say to the horses: *"Come and play with us, we have many fine games, we will race with you, come catch us."* And with that the colts kicked up their heels flicked their tails and raced across the open field. But when they looked back and saw the horses were not following they were puzzled. They knew nothing of the harnesses and could not understand why the horses did not want to play. So they called to them: *"Why do you not race with us? Are you tired? Are you too weak? Do you not have strength to run? You are much too solemn, you need more joy in life."* But the horses answered not a word nor did they stamp their feet or toss their heads. But they stood, quiet and still, waiting for the voice of the Master.

Again the colts called to them: *"Why do you stand so in the hot sun? Come over here in the shade of this nice tree. See how green the grass is? You must be hungry, come and feed with us, it is so green and so good. You look thirsty, come drink of one of our many streams of cool, clear water."* But the horses answered them not so much as a glance but stood still waiting for the command to go forward with the King.

Colts in the Master's Corral

And then the scene changed and I saw lariat nooses fall around the necks of the two colts and they were led off to the Master's corral for training and discipline. How sad they were as the lovely green fields disappeared and they were put into the confinement of the corral with its brown dirt and high fence. The colts ran from fence to fence seeking freedom but found that they were confined to this place of training. And then the Trainer began to work on them with His whip and His bridle. What a death for those who had been all their lives accustomed to such a freedom! They could not understand the reason for this torture, this terrible discipline. What crime had they done to deserve this? Little did they know of the responsibility that was to be theirs when they had submitted to the discipline, learned to perfectly obey the Master and finished their training. All they knew was that this processing was the most horrible thing they had ever known.

Submission and Rebellion

One of the colts rebelled under the training and said, *"This is not for me. I like my freedom, my green hills, my flowing streams of fresh water. I will not take any more of this confinement, this terrible training."* So he found a way out, jumped the fence and ran happily back to the meadows of grass. I was astonished that the Master let him go and went not after him. But He devoted His attention to the remaining colt. This colt, though he had the same opportunity to escape, decided to submit his own will and learn the ways of the Master. The training got harder than ever but he was rapidly learning more and more how to obey the slightest wish of the Master and to respond to even the quietness of His voice. And I saw that had there been no training, no testing, there would have been neither submission nor rebellion from either of the colts. For in the field they did not have the choice to rebel or submit, they were sinless in their innocence. But when brought to the place of testing and training and discipline, then was made manifest the obedience of one and the rebellion of the other. And though it seemed safer not to come to the place of discipline because of the risk of being found rebellious, yet I saw that without this there could be no sharing of His glory, no Sonship.

Into the Harness

Finally this period of training was over. Was he now rewarded with his freedom and sent back to the fields? Oh no. But a greater confinement than ever now took place as a harness dropped about his shoulders. Now he found there was not even the freedom to run about the small corral for in the harness he could only move where and when his Master spoke. And unless the Master spoke he stood still.

The scene changed and I saw the other colt standing on the side of a hill nibbling at some grass. Then across the fields, down the road came the King's carriage drawn by six horses. With amazement he saw that in the lead, on the right side, was his brother colt now made strong and mature on the good corn in the Master's stable. He saw the lovely pom-poms shaking in the wind, noticed the glittering gold-bordered harness about his brother, heard the beautiful tinkling of the bells on his feet – and envy came into his heart. Thus he complained to himself: *"Why has my brother been so honored, and I am neglected? They have not put bells on MY feet nor pom-poms on MY head. The Master has not given ME the* wonderful responsibility of pulling His carriage, has not put about ME the gold harness. Why have they chosen my brother instead of me?" And by the Spirit the answer came back to me as I watched: "Because one submitted to the will and discipline of the Master and one rebelled, thus has one been chosen and the other set aside."

A Famine in the Land

Then I saw a great drought sweep across the countryside and the green grass became dead, dry, brown and brittle. The little streams of water dried up, stopped flowing, and there was only a small, muddy puddle here and there. I saw the little colt (I was amazed that it never seemed to grow or mature) as he ran here and there across the fields looking for fresh streams and green pastures finding none. Still he ran, seemingly in circles, always looking for something to feed his famished spirit. But there was a famine in the land and the rich green pastures and flowing streams of yesterday were not to be had. And one day the colt stood on the hillside on weak and wobbly legs wondering where to go next to find food and how to get strength to go. It seemed like there was no use, for good food and flowing streams were a thing of the past and all the efforts to find more only taxed his waning strength. Suddenly he saw the King's carriage coming down the road pulled by six great horses. And he saw his brother, fat and strong, muscles rippling, sleek and beautiful with much grooming. His heart was amazed and perplexed, and he cried out: *"My brother where do you find the food to keep you strong and fat in these days of famine? I have run everywhere in my freedom, searching for food, and I find none. Where do you in your awful confinement find food in this time of drought? Tell me, please, for I must know!"* And then the answer came back from a voice filled with victory and praise: *"In my Master's House there is a secret place in the confining limitations of His stables where He feeds me by His own hand and His granaries never run empty and His well never runs dry."*

And with this the Lord made me to know that in the day when people are weak and famished in their spirits in the time of spiritual famine that those who have lost their own wills and have come into the secret place of the most High into the utter confinement of His perfect will shall have plenty of the corn of Heaven and a never ending flow of fresh streams of revelation by His Spirit.

Thus the vision ended.

Interpretation of the Vision

"Write the vision, and make it plain upon tables, that he may run that readeth it," (Habakkuk 2:2). *"Harness the horses; and get up, ye horseman,"* (Jeremiah 46:4). I am sure that many of you who can hear what the Spirit saith to the Church have already seen what God was showing in the vision. But let me make it plain. Being born into the Family of God feeding in the green pastures and drinking of the many streams of the unfolding revelation of His purposes is fine and wonderful. But it is not enough. While we were children, young and undisciplined, limited only by the outer fence of the Law that ran around the limits of the pastures (that kept us from getting into the dark pastures of poison weeds), He was content to watch us develop and grow into young manhood, spiritually speaking. But the time came to those who fed in His pastures and drank at His streams, when they were to be brought into discipline or "child-training" for the purpose of making them mature sons. Many of the children today cannot understand why some of those who have put on the harness of God cannot get excited by the many religious games and the playful antics of the immature. They wonder why the disciplined ones run not after every new revelation or feed on every opportunity to engage in seemingly "good and profitable" religious activities. They wonder why some will not race with them in their frantic efforts to build great works and great and notable ministries. They cannot understand the simple fact that this company of saints is waiting for the voice of the Master and they do not hear God in all this outward

activity. They will move in their time when the Master speaks. But not before, though many temptations come from the playful colts. And the colts cannot understand why those who seemingly appear to have great abilities and strength are not putting it to good use. "Get the carriage on the road," they say, but the disciplined ones, those in God's harness, know better than to move before they hear the voice of the Master. They will move in their time with purpose and great responsibility.

And the Lord made me to know that there were many whom He had brought into training who had rebelled against the discipline, the chastising of the Father. They could not be trusted with the great responsibility of mature sonship so He let them go back to their freedom, back to their religious activities and revelations and gifts. They are still His people, still feeding in His pastures, but He has set them aside from the great purposes for this end of the age. So they revel in their freedom feeling that they were the chosen ones with the many streams of living water not knowing that they have been set aside as unfit for His great work in this end of the age.

He showed me that though the chastising seemeth grievous for the time and the discipline hard to endure yet the result with all the glory of sonship is worth it all and the glory to follow far exceeds the suffering we endure. And though some lose even their lives in this training yet they will share alike in the glory of His eternal purposes. So faint not saints of God for it is the Lord that doth bring thee into confinement and not thine enemy. It is for thy good and for His glory so endure all things with praises and thanksgiving that He hath counted thee worthy to share His glory! Fear thou not the whip in His hand for it is not to punish thee but to correct and train thee that thou mightest come into submission to His will and be found in His likeness in that hour. Rejoice thou in thy trials in all thy tribulations and glory thou in His cross and in the confining limitations of His harness for He hath chosen thee and He hath taken upon Himself the responsibility of keeping thee strong and well fed. So lean thou upon Him and trust not in thine own ability and thine own understanding. So shalt thou be fed and His hand shall be upon thee and His glory shall overshadow thee and shall flow through thee as it goes forth to cover the earth. Glory to God! Bless the Lord! He's wonderful! Let Him be Lord of your life, friends, and complain not at that which He bringeth to pass in your life.

Plenty in the Time of Famine

For in the hour when famine sweeps the land He shall feed by His own hand those who are submitted to His perfect will and who dwell in the secret place of the Most High. When terror stalks the land those in His harness shall not be afraid for they shall feel His bit and bridle and know the guidance of His Spirit. When others are weak and frail and fearful, there shall be those who shall be strong in the power of His might and shall lack for no good thing. In the hour when the traditions of the religious systems have proven false and their streams have dried up, then His chosen ones shall speak forth with the true Word of the Lord. So rejoice, sons of God, that you have been chosen by His grace for this great work in this last hour.

The fence which kept the colts in their own meadows and their own pastures mean nothing to the team in the harness for the gates open to them and they go forth pulling the King's carriage into many strange and wonderful places. They do not stop to eat the poison weeds of sin for they feed only in the Master's stable. These fields they trample under their feet as they go forth on the King's business. And so to those who are brought into absolute subjection to His will there is no Law. For they move in the Grace of God led only by His Spirit where all things are lawful but not all things are expedient. This is a dangerous realm for the undisciplined and many have perished in sin as they leaped over the fence without His harness and His bridle. Some have thought of themselves as being completely harnessed and submissive to Him only to find that in some avenue of their life there dwelled rebellion and self-will. Let us wait before Him until He puts His noose around us and draws us to His place of training. And let us learn of the dealings of God and the movings of His Spirit until at last we feel His harness drop about us and hear His voice guiding us. Then there is safety from the traps and pitfalls of sin and then shall we abide in His House forever!

These are the unchanging ways of God: preparation and proving precede leadership.

- Moses spent 40 years in the wilderness before he was released as a leader.
- Joseph spent years in prison before he ruled Egypt.
- David lived in the wilderness for years before he was trusted to rule Israel.
- John the Baptist grew up in the wilderness, spending almost 30 years in preparation for a ministry that only lasted for about 6 months.[23]
- Paul underwent extensive preparation before he was finally commissioned as an apostle.
- Jesus' disciples were all personally prepared and proven by Jesus before He entrusted them with the leadership of His church.
- The Lord Jesus Himself "increased in wisdom and stature, and in favour with God and man" (Luke 2:52), and "learned obedience from what he suffered" (Heb. 5:8).

Thus, Paul instructs us that a novice should not be given primary leadership responsibility:

> He must not be a recent convert, or he may become conceited and fall under the same judgment as the devil. (1 Tim. 3:6)

---

[23] Today we do just the opposite. We spend 6 months in preparation for a ministry of 30 years!

We will ignore this prohibition at our own risk! Emerging leaders must be given time to learn, to be proven, to learn discipline and to be broken, in order for character to be formed. Moreover, they must also learn that faithfulness in a little is required before they will receive responsibility for much:

> *Whoever can be trusted with very little can also be trusted with much, and whoever is dishonest with very little will also be dishonest with much. (Luke 16:10)*

Accountability

Furthermore, the emerging leader must learn to choose accountability. To be accountable means to be responsible to others, to allow others to call one to account. An unaccountable person, on the other hand, will answer to no one outside of himself.

> The word "accountability" in English comes from the fourteenth century word *accounts,* meaning a record of money received and paid. King James II of England was the first to publicly use the term "accountability." In 1688 he said to his people, "I am accountable for all things that I openly and voluntarily do or say."
>
> In short, the word means being answerable for your actions. It does not necessarily mean you will succeed. James lost his throne within a year of making his pledge – due to religious quarrels! Nevertheless, accountability offers something better than success. It provides a measure of whether you are doing the best you can in the circumstances, important information however well you do.[24]

Jesus, of course, was accountable. He lived and ministered under the authority of His heavenly Father:

---

[24] From *Accountable Leadership* by Paul Chaffee (1993), pp. 8-9.

...I do nothing on my own but speak just what the Father has taught me. (John 8:28)

By myself I can do nothing; I judge only as I hear, and my judgment is just, for I seek not to please myself but him who sent me. (John 5:30)

Although he was a son, he learned obedience from what he suffered (Heb. 5:8)

Moreover, as a child, He was also accountable to His earthly parents:

Then he went down to Nazareth with them and was obedient to them... (Luke 2:51)

By His example, Jesus taught that in order to have true authority, one must first be under authority.

The centurion in Matthew 8 was accountable: "I myself am a man under authority" (v. 9). In that state of being "under authority" he exercised authority: "with soldiers under me. I tell this one, 'Go,' and he goes; and that one, 'Come,' and he comes. I say to my servant, 'Do this,' and he does it" (v. 9). The centurion exercised sound authority because he was first under authority. Consequently he was able to recognize the true authority of Jesus: "just say the word, and my servant will be healed" (v. 8).

Even Paul, the great apostle, was accountable in his ministry.

... we have renounced secret and shameful ways; we do not use deception, nor do we distort the word of God. On the contrary, by setting forth the truth plainly we commend ourselves to every man's conscience in the sight of God. (2 Cor. 4:2;cf. 6:3)

Too often, people think of Paul as an independent ministry, accountable to no one but God. But Paul was sent out by the church at Antioch (Acts 13:3) and he remained accountable to that spiritual community throughout his ministry (Acts 14:26-28; 15:2-3, 35-40; 18:22-23). Moreover, Paul willingly made himself accountable to the leaders of the church at Jerusalem, from whom the gospel had come initially (Acts 21:17-26; cf. Gal. 2:2). Paul deliberately chose accountability in the issue of finances:

> We want to avoid any criticism of the way we administer this liberal gift. For we are taking pains to do what is right, not only in the eyes of the Lord but also in the eyes of men. (2 Cor. 8:20-21; cf. 1 Cor. 9:12)

Accountability is central to character and to effective leadership. Leaders are given trust by their communities. To accept a leadership role is to receive trust from one's community. The task of Christian leadership comes with high standards – the highest, we would hope! Thus, some form of accountability must be in place to measure whether or not such standards are being adhered to by the leader and whether the trust his community has given him is being honored or abused.

> Now it is required that those who have been given a trust must prove faithful. (1 Cor. 4:2)

The following are some areas of accountability that should be maintained in a leader's life and ministry:

- Integrity of life – truthfulness in word, purity in thought, and honesty in action. High moral and ethical standards of behavior.
- Integrity of motive – seeking the highest good of the community before his own benefit.
- Integrity of finance – abstaining from personal gain in community matters and providing appropriate reports.
- Integrity of organization – ensuring that right systems and relationships are in place and maintained in his or her organization both within (e.g., accounting, legal systems all in place) and without (e.g., relationships with the government).
- Integrity of doctrine – all teaching and doctrinal positions must be sound.

- Integrity of decisions regarding the community – putting the will of God first before all temporal expediency and gain.
- Integrity of relationships – working through conflict with people and not using one's position of power to settle personal issues.
- Integrity of accountability – relationships of genuine accountability must be in place, not merely the form of them.

Every leader at every level must be genuinely accountable in all these areas. Healthy leaders will be accountable ones!

However, in certain cultures it is very difficult for the "top" leader in an organization to be accountable to someone else within his own organization. A top leader who does not presently have a relationship of accountability built into the system of his community should seek an outside relationship of accountability. The actual process of doing this could look something like the following:

1. Prayerfully, find a person to whom you can be accountable. This person must be:

   a. Trusted by you and by your spiritual community.
   b. Knowledgeable about your life and ministry environment.
   c. Of stature in your eyes (not someone you can intimidate) and in the eyes of your community (their trust for him will bring stability and strength to the community).
   d. Accessible both to you and to other leaders in your community.

2. Ask the person to pray about entering into this relationship with you. You will probably need to ask him several times. A worthy person will likely not quickly enter into such a relationship without being assured of your genuine desire for it and your willingness to submit to the guidelines.

3. When he positively responds, meet with him to establish guidelines for the relationship:

    a. How often you will meet and where.
    b. The content of your meetings.
    c. Who else from your community should have access to him and how that should happen.
    d. On what conditions the relationship should be ended if that should ever be required.
    e. How often the guidelines should be revisited for relevancy and suitability.

    Mutual expectations should be made very clear up front.

4. Once the guidelines for the relationship are agreed upon and formally established between you, then the relationship should be presented to your community. The knowledge that their top leader is in a genuinely accountable relationship will bring peace and stability to the community.

5. The guidelines for the relationship should then be maintained – if well-designed, they will form the basis for a healthy and fruitful friendship.

6. Periodically, the person you're accountable to should meet with your community or with its main leaders to give them an opportunity to talk to him and maintain their relationships with him.

A leader with godly character will not fear accountability but will rather choose it. Where there is unaccountability and independence in a leader's life, there will be trouble – sooner or later! An unaccountable leader is a dangerous leader; moreover, the more gifted he is, the more dangerous he is!

What Character Is Not

To help define what character is, we should also examine what it is not: [25]

1. Character is not just what a person will ideally be in the future. Character is what a person is at this present time. When pressure comes to a person's life, the real person surfaces. A person may act and think one way under the blessings of the Lord, but quite another way when the trials and heat of life are his portion.

2. Character is not only how a person acts. Character also includes a person's inner thoughts, motives and attitudes. Thoughts, though hidden, indicate the real character of a person. Motives, too, are true expressions of the inner man. To change the character of a person, one must go deeper than action.

3. Character does not appear without pressure. The pressures of life test what the Lord has really accomplished in a person's character. When the heat is upon a person's character, his true character surfaces. The common irritations of everyday living expose the weaknesses in every person's life. How do you respond to the disappointments and pressures of everyday life? Character is formed under such pressures and circumstances. The qualities that are truly part of a person's character are consistent, whether the heat is on or off his life.

4. Character is not only that which other people see on the outside. Character is what other people do not see. People may see only the side of a person that a person wants to display, but God sees the real person. An individual cannot hide his weaknesses from the Lord. Man may look

---

[25] Adapted from *The Making of a Leader* by Frank Damazio.

at the externals, but the Lord looks at the heart. The Lord commands good works from each one of us, but these must proceed out of a godly character. A person can do many outward religious works, and still be ungodly. Works are not always a sign of good character.

5. Character is not limited to having wisdom to comment on the behavior of others. Intellectually knowing how to act, think and feel consistently with Bible principles may be a far cry from actually living in harmony with those principles. A person with true character doesn't just tell other people what to do, but lives as an example worthy of following.

6. Character is not limited to relationships between Christians. To believe that it does not matter how a Christian acts toward non-Christians is a deception. Character shows forth godly principles in every situation and toward all people. For example, a Christian worker must give the same respect to an employer whether he is Christian or not.

7. Character is not limited to a person's relationship with his spiritual family. It also shows in how he treats his natural family. A Christian must demonstrate his faith and love in the way he treats his immediate family. A person's character can be discerned by the way he respects and honors his mother and father. A Christian with an unbelieving natural family can win his family to Christ by having a mature, loving character toward them.

Thus, from inward union with Jesus, lived out in the daily context of the community – in the family, the church, the leadership team and the world – God forms character. This is character of a quality that He can trust – character that has been refined in the fire.

To a man or woman of character, God can entrust a calling.

chapter 5

Calling

A leader must have a calling and a vision from God or else he would be wise not to lead (Jam. 3:1). Like all true leaders at any level of responsibility, Paul was "sent not from men nor by man, but by Jesus Christ and God the Father" (Gal. 1:1). There is no substitute for the Divine call in the leader's life. A leader may have impeccable character, a great desire to be a leader and strong technical abilities to lead and manage; but without a Divine vision he will have nowhere to take his followers and he will accomplish little of lasting value (John 15:4-6).

Strong calling, however, must not be disconnected from a deep surrender to and relationship with Christ. Christ comes first! Dietrich Bonhoeffer warned:

> God hates visionary dreaming; it makes the dreamer proud and pretentious. The man who fashions a visionary ideal of community demands that it be realized by God, by others, and by himself. He enters the community of Christians with his demands, sets up his own law, and judges the brethren and God Himself accordingly.... He acts as if he is the creator of the Christian community, as if his dream binds men together. When things do not go his way, he calls the effort a failure. When his ideal picture is destroyed, he sees the community going to smash. So he becomes, first an accuser of his brethren, then an accuser of God, and finally the despairing accuser of himself. *(Life Together)*

> *For in the multitude of dreams and many words there is also vanity. But fear God. (Eccl. 5:7)*

A true calling comes from God. Then it becomes the leader's own vision, something he can share passionately with others. Without the Divine initiation, however, man's vision is mere human ambition.

The following graphic contrasts a healthy vision with human ambition.

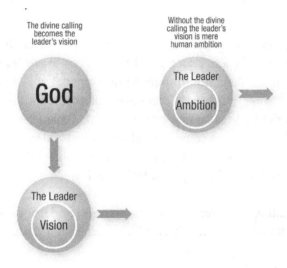

The calling must come originally from Christ and be received in the integrity of the leader's heart. Left to himself, man's vision will often contain a mixture. He might have a genuine calling from God, but there will often be much of himself mixed in with it too. This is one reason why God allows us (like Joseph and Moses) to go through sufferings – to purify our hearts from mixture (1 Pet. 1:6-7).

Thomas Merton wrote about zealous human ambition:

> We must be on our guard against a kind of blind and immature zeal – the zeal of the enthusiast or the zealot – which represents precisely a frantic compensation for the deeply personal qualities which are lacking to us. The zealot is man who "loses himself" in his cause in such a way that he can no longer "find himself" at all. Yet paradoxically this "loss" of himself is not the salutary self-forgetfulness commanded by Christ. It is rather an immersion

in his own willfulness conceived of as the will of an abstract, non-personal force: the force of a project or program. *(Seasons of Celebration)*

In addition, the calling must be submitted to community. It is only as the leader is genuinely accountable to his community and allows them to help mold and clarify his calling that he is assured of purity of vision. Thus, the calling of the leader must be birthed in Christ, purified in community and built upon fire-tested character.

In contrast to true leadership that comes from union with God, Korah appointed *himself* to be a leader (Num. 16–17). The following characterized his leadership:

1. He caused others to rise up against existing spiritual authority (Num. 16:2).
2. He publicly criticized and questioned the existing leadership (Num. 16:3).
3. He accused the leadership of what he himself was guilty (Num. 16:3).
4. He was not satisfied with the position he was given. He wanted more authority and a higher position (Num. 16:10).
5. He continually murmured against the Divinely-appointed leadership (Num. 16:11).
6. He ended under the judgment of God (Num. 16:31-35).

In one sense, Saul was appointed by *man* to be a leader. The Lord told Samuel to give them what they wanted – a man to rule over them (1 Sam. 8–10). Then Samuel warned the people that their new leader was destined to rob and spoil them (1 Sam. 8:11-17). It was significant that Samuel anointed Saul with oil poured from a man-made flask (1 Sam. 10:1), whereas he anointed David (God's choice) with the horn of an animal (1 Sam. 16:13) that was not made by man.

Today, man-appointed leaders look upon Christian leadership as a profession or a career. They are more concerned with the medical benefits or retirement accounts that come with the "job" than they are for the sheep of God. They are the "hired hands" (John 10:12-13). They are religious professionals who do not further the life of God's people.

In contrast to both self-appointed and man-appointed leadership, true leadership will be appointed by God.

> *Paul, an apostle – sent not from men nor by man, but by Jesus Christ and God the Father, who raised him from the dead (Gal. 1:1)*

True spiritual leadership does not come from loyalty to one's denomination, or from some personal vested interest in leading – it comes from God.

Marks of the Divine Call

Leaders will be aware of the call of God on their lives. They may fight or deny the call for a while, but they will still know God has called them:

> *For if I preach the gospel, I have nothing to boast of, for necessity is laid upon me; yes, woe is me if I do not preach the gospel! For if I do this willingly, I have a reward; but if against my will, I have been entrusted with a stewardship. (1 Cor. 9:16-17)*

> *After much discussion, Peter got up and addressed them: "Brothers, you know that some time ago God made a choice among you that the Gentiles might hear from my lips the message of the gospel and believe." (Acts 15:7)*

Another way we can discern a true Divine call to leadership upon a man's life is by seeing if people are actually experiencing personal *transformation* through their interaction with him. That is proof of his calling from God.

You yourselves are our letter, written on our hearts, known and read by everybody. You show that you are a letter from Christ, the result of our ministry, written not with ink but with the Spirit of the living God, not on tablets of stone but on tablets of human hearts. (2 Cor. 3:2-3)

For what is our hope, our joy, or the crown in which we will glory in the presence of our Lord Jesus when he comes? Is it not you? Indeed, you are our glory and joy. (1 Thess. 2:19-20)

The Calling Collage

One's individual calling will be the result of a very complex interaction between the following elements in the leader's life:

- Personality: people may have similar callings, but their approaches are entirely different based upon their very different personalities. God uses these differences in fulfilling His own purposes.
- Culture: we are all deeply influenced by our own cultures.
- Gender: gender will influence our callings.
- Age: as we grow, our callings change, develop and mature.
- Physical condition: if you're called to evangelize the remote tribes on a high mountain, you had better be physically fit! Your physical condition will usually fit your calling.
- Leader/manager orientation: are you a long-term, big picture thinker or more of a short-term, detail thinker?
- Genes: what abilities and orientations were you born with?
- Life experiences: we discern God's purposes through understanding the experiences of our lives.
- Relationships: our relationships with others can profoundly influence our own callings.
- Role models: who are your role models that you admire and emulate?
- Mentors: who are the mentors who have profoundly impacted your life?

- Family heritage: we are not isolated individuals, but our lives stand on the lives of those in our families before us bringing continuity and fulfillment.
- Current family (spouse, children, relatives): what are their complementary callings, what are their attitudes and positions that influence us?
- Spiritual gifts: what supernatural gifts of 1 Corinthians 12 do you have?
- Motivational gifts: what are your motivational gifts of Romans 12, etc.?
- Ministry gifts: do you have any of the five ministry gifts of Ephesians 4?
- Formal education: your level of education may have a significant influence on your calling.
- Training experiences: throughout your life you will undergo training of various kinds that may influence your calling.

Thus, there are not only five specific callings (e.g., Ephesians 4) but an almost infinite number of callings that match each individual perfectly in the purposes of God.

Consequently, it is not sufficient merely to do some simplistic "gift assessment." Instead, we must design relationships, experiences and reflective exercises that help emerging leaders to understand how this very complicated collage fits together in their lives.

A Divine calling to lead establishes the leader's purpose, passion and commission.

Purpose

Without a clear understanding of his purpose,[26] the leader will not accomplish much. He will be like the man who shoots his gun while aiming at nothing; of course, he's sure to hit it!

The author once attended a seminar held by a popular teacher on leadership. At that seminar there were leaders from all religious backgrounds, including several cults! It is fruitless and counter-productive to try to teach leadership principles to people who do not actually possess a genuine calling and vision from God to lead. Leadership is not merely a set of principles that will help you influence people; leadership primarily involves the reality of where you will lead them. It is not just the "how;" it is most importantly the "where." Many contemporary leadership teachers mistakenly presuppose that the people who attend their seminars and read their books are actually called of God to lead. The truth is: if you do not have a clear Divine calling, you should not try to lead – you will hurt both yourself (Jam. 3:1) and others.

> *Not many of you should presume to be teachers, my brothers, because you know that we who teach will be judged more strictly. (Jam. 3:1)*

Certainly James' words apply to leaders, too – they will be judged more strictly because of their influence on the lives of others!

Leaders must have a clear purpose for their leadership, and this purpose must be established by God. We must pursue His will; not "leadership success" for its own sake.

Moreover, having a clear understanding of his calling will allow the leader to focus and be more effective (e.g., Ex. 18:13-26; 2 Cor. 10:13-18).

---

[26] Please see *Purpose* by Malcolm Webber for more on how to know God's will.

Passion

With a vision of Divine purpose comes the courage and dedication to fulfill that purpose. A leader who is surrendered to Jesus' lordship will commit his all to obey the specific calling Jesus gave him.

The way is frequently hard (Acts 14:22); only the truly committed will make it. Leadership is risky work. It can be unpopular. It will always involve some significant personal costs to the leader himself. The leader needs the courage that only comes from confidence in the Divine call.

Moreover, only those who can passionately communicate the exciting possibilities of the future will be able to persuade others to follow them down a frequently difficult path. People need strong visionary leadership to help them start moving and to keep on moving. People sacrifice for a passionate vision.

Commission

In the leader's life, there will be a specific time of Divine commission when he is set apart for the work to which God has called him. For example, in Acts 13, Paul was set apart for his apostolic ministry:

> In the church at Antioch there were prophets and teachers: Barnabas, Simeon called Niger, Lucius of Cyrene, Manaen (who had been brought up with Herod the tetrarch) and Saul. While they were worshiping the Lord and fasting, the Holy Spirit said, "Set apart for me Barnabas and Saul for the work to which I have called them." So after they had fasted and prayed, they placed their hands on them and sent them off. The two of them, sent on their way by the Holy Spirit, went down to Seleucia and sailed from there to Cyprus. (Acts 13:1-4)

Paul was called to this ministry a long time before,[27] and he would no doubt have experienced the manifestation of many apostolic giftings in his life previous to this time. However, he did not have apostolic *authority* until he was commissioned to this ministry.

This commission was given by the Holy Spirit ("sent on their way by the Holy Spirit"; Acts 13:4; cf. Matt. 9:38; 1 Cor. 1:1; Gal. 1:1; Deut. 31:14) in the context of the authority structure of the church ("they placed their hands on them and sent them off", Acts 13:3; cf. Acts 6:3-6; 15:28). Thus, the calling comes from God and is then confirmed by the community. This commission establishes and affirms the leader's right to lead – to himself as well as to his constituency.

Every leader was called to his ministry before the foundation of the world:

> *For he chose us in him before the creation of the world… (Eph. 1:4)*

> *Before I formed you in the womb I knew you, before you were born I set you apart; I appointed you as a prophet to the nations. (Jer. 1:5; cf. 2 Tim. 1:9)*

This calling then becomes known to the leader at some point in his life. For example, God revealed something of Paul's calling to him at the time of his salvation:

> *…This man is my chosen instrument to carry my name before the Gentiles and their kings and before the people of Israel. I will show him how much he must suffer for my name. (Acts 9:15-16)*

> *Now get up and stand on your feet. I have appeared to you to appoint you as a servant and as a witness of what you have seen of me and what I will show you. I will rescue you from your own*

---

[27] In reality, Paul was called to apostolic ministry before the foundation of the world, and then he discovered his calling on the road to Damascus.

people and from the Gentiles. I am sending you to them to open their eyes and turn them from darkness to light, and from the power of Satan to God, so that they may receive forgiveness of sins and a place among those who are sanctified by faith in me. (Acts 26:16-18)

The commission then comes at a certain time and constitutes the leader's "marching orders." Certainly the leader will previously be aware that he has the specific calling of God on his life and he will likely experience the manifestation of certain gifts associated with that calling. But he has not yet been commissioned, so he does not yet possess Divine authority for his ministry.

Here is where some emerging leaders make an error. They know that God has called them to a certain ministry and they function to some extent in gifts associated with that ministry. But they err when they begin to assume they have the authority of that ministry before they are actually commissioned. Authority does not come from gifting; it comes from the commission.

Here is the Divine order: the calling limits the commission and the commission limits the authority – it establishes boundaries. You may have a larger calling from God that you will ultimately fulfill, but until you have been specifically commissioned, you do not yet have the authority of that calling. Your authority is limited by your commission. This defines your present "field" of ministry:

> *We, however, will not boast beyond proper limits, but will confine our boasting to the field God has assigned to us, a field that reaches even to you. (2 Cor. 10:13)*

Authority does not simply proceed from gifting. You may have giftings in many areas, but until you have been specifically commissioned in those areas your authority is limited.[28]

As you are faithful in what He gives you to do, God might expand your field of ministry (Luke 16:10). Paul faithfully taught for years before receiving his apostolic commission.

Furthermore, this commission must be inspired by the direction of the Holy Spirit and not just be a response to an organizational need or vision. Too often we appoint men to fulfill organizational needs without spending the necessary time before God to know for sure that it is *His* purpose and timing. This is why many men fail – they are promoted to higher levels of leadership in response to a human need or vision but they are not called to those responsibilities or gifted for them. The Holy Spirit initiated Paul's commission in Acts 13 – it was not merely a human response to the need for the gospel to be preached in new areas.

Since the leader now has a calling from God, he therefore needs the specific competencies to be able to fulfill that calling. This brings us to the fifth "C."

---

[28] The specific nature of this commissioning will vary, depending on the nature of the calling. Not every calling needs a formal public commissioning. But for there to be appropriate authority that comes with a calling, the community must recognize and affirm the calling.

chapter 6

Competencies

A leader may possess a burning vision and a holy character, but without the technical abilities to lead, he will be followed by confusion and frustration; and the greater the vision, the greater the confusion.

This is where many Christian leaders fail. They have a good knowledge of the Bible, but they have never learned how to lead people or manage the practical aspects of an organization. They have a genuine vision and strong character, but they lack basic leadership skills.

Other leaders do have good strategic and technical abilities to lead, but they lack sound biblical knowledge. They are able to build a large, and apparently successful, church or ministry, but they lead it into spiritual error. Again, the issue is inadequate competencies (2 Tim. 3:14-17).

Paul told Timothy to choose elders who had some basic organizational competencies:

> *He must manage his own family well and see that his children obey him with proper respect. (If anyone does not know how to manage his own family, how can he take care of God's church?) (1 Tim. 3:4-5)*

This was in contrast to the false leaders at Ephesus who did not know what they were doing:

> *They want to be teachers of the law, but they do not know what they are talking about or what they so confidently affirm. (1 Tim. 1:7)*

Thus, the leader must "know how" to do it. It is not enough to just be blown along by the Holy Spirit. This capacity includes the ability to understand, to teach and to appropriately use the Word of God:

> *Do your best to present yourself to God as one approved, a workman who does not need to be ashamed and who correctly handles the word of truth. (2 Tim. 2:15; cf. 2 Tim. 4:2)*

In spite of the fact that most of our Bible schools and seminaries focus on biblical knowledge in their training processes, according to a recent study, a great number of Christian leaders are not well-equipped in the Scriptures.[29]

Please notice that the ConneXions model speaks of "competencies" rather than "knowledge of the Word of God." This emphasizes that our goal in leader development is not merely someone who *knows* the Word, but a Christian leader who is actually *doing* the Word (cf. Jam. 2:14-26; John 5:39-40). This distinguishes the ConneXions model from the traditional approach to leader development which emphasizes knowledge for its own sake. Our goal in leader development should not be mere intellectual knowledge, but wisdom – the capacity to use knowledge in a fruitful way.

To fulfill the requirements of his calling, the Christian leader will also need supernatural gifts in addition to natural, human abilities.

> *...the land of Egypt is before you; settle your father and your brothers in the best part of the land. Let them live in Goshen. And if you know of any among them with special ability, put them in charge of my own livestock. (Gen. 47:6)*

---

[29] According to a 2003 study by the Barna Research Group, only 51 percent of Christian ministers in the U.S., representing a random cross-section of Protestant churches, have a biblical view on six core beliefs (the accuracy of biblical teaching, the sinless nature of Jesus, the literal existence of Satan, the omnipotence and omniscience of God, salvation by grace alone and the personal responsibility to evangelize).

See, I have chosen Bezalel son of Uri, the son of Hur, of the tribe of Judah, and I have filled him with the Spirit of God, with skill, ability and knowledge in all kinds of crafts – to make artistic designs for work in gold, silver and bronze, to cut and set stones, to work in wood, and to engage in all kinds of craftsmanship. Moreover, I have appointed Oholiab son of Ahisamach, of the tribe of Dan, to help him. Also I have given skill to all the craftsmen to make everything I have commanded you: (Ex. 31:2-6)

King Solomon sent to Tyre and brought Huram, whose mother was a widow from the tribe of Naphtali and whose father was a man of Tyre and a craftsman in bronze. Huram was highly skilled and experienced in all kinds of bronze work. He came to King Solomon and did all the work assigned to him. (1 Kings 7:13-14)

…seventeen hundred able men – were responsible in Israel west of the Jordan for all the work of the LORD and for the king's service… a search was made in the records, and capable men among the Hebronites were found at Jazer in Gilead. Jeriah had twenty-seven hundred relatives, who were able men and heads of families, and King David put them in charge… for every matter pertaining to God and for the affairs of the king. (1 Chron. 26:30-32)

this Ezra came up from Babylon. He was a teacher well versed in the Law of Moses, which the LORD, the God of Israel, had given… Ezra had devoted himself to the study and observance of the Law of the LORD, and to teaching its decrees and laws in Israel. (Ezra 7:6-10)

And David shepherded them with integrity of heart; with skillful hands he led them. (Ps. 78:72)

Do you see a man skilled in his work? He will serve before kings; he will not serve before obscure men. (Prov. 22:29)

Brothers, choose seven men from among you who are known to be full of the Spirit and wisdom. We will turn this responsibility over to them (Acts 6:3)

I am not ashamed of the gospel, because it is the power of God for the salvation of everyone who believes: first for the Jew, then for the Gentile. (Rom. 1:16)

We have different gifts, according to the grace given us. If a man's gift is prophesying, let him use it in proportion to his faith. If it is serving, let him serve; if it is teaching, let him teach; if it is encouraging, let him encourage; if it is contributing to the needs of others, let him give generously; if it is leadership, let him govern diligently; if it is showing mercy, let him do it cheerfully. (Rom. 12:6-8)

Now to each one the manifestation of the Spirit is given for the common good. (1 Cor. 12:7)

...our gospel came to you not simply with words, but also with power, with the Holy Spirit and with deep conviction... (1 Thess. 1:5)

Moreover, he also needs experience in ministry before he is commissioned. His spiritual community, of course, is the safe context in which he should "practice" as he grows as an emerging leader.

As the leader matures, he will experience changes in tasks and responsibilities. His field of leadership may become not only bigger but also more difficult. Higher leadership responsibilities require different, and often more sophisticated, competencies. Consequently, the growing leader will need different and more advanced competencies. He will need to embrace an attitude of continuous learning in his life. He will also need ongoing mentoring by a variety of older leaders.

There are many kinds of competencies that are necessary for leaders to have. Naturally, individual leaders will probably not be expert in every competency; thus, the need for a well-rounded team. Essentially, the individual's calling defines his necessary competencies. So, for example, a teacher of the Word needs to have studied some Hebrew and Greek, but an evangelist does not.

Building Competencies

There are four stages of learning new competencies:

1. The initial gaining of the knowledge or skill.

    This involves teaching or self-study. This stage can also involve some kind of initial assessment to see what the emerging learner already knows.

2. Increased knowledge or skill proficiency.

    The emerging leader's competencies are increased in this stage through case studies, modeling and practice.

3. Ability to apply knowledge or skills in simple situations.

    This can involve on-the-job mentoring as well as appropriate challenging assignments.

4. Ability to apply knowledge or skill in increasingly complex situations.

    Now the emerging leader is involved in complex situations where he must solve problems and react to changing circumstances. In addition, he needs feedback on his performance.

In these four stages, the emerging leader moves from reception of facts to active and sophisticated application of them.

Competence is the last part of our model of a healthy leader. It is absolutely necessary that a leader have strong competencies.

chapter 7

Observations and Applications Regarding the ConneXions Model

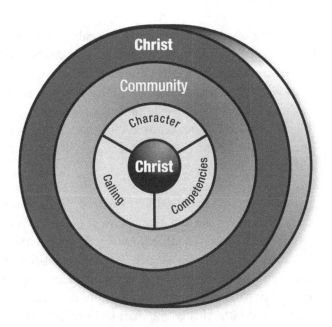

The following are some general observations and practical applications regarding the ConneXions model:

1. Too often, in leader development, we only deal with competencies. When a young man or woman goes to Bible school to become a leader, what is addressed? Competencies! Perhaps some token attention is paid to the other four elements, but for the most part, our attention to "leader development" is given in the area of competencies such as biblical knowledge, how to preach, how to counsel, etc.

   Competencies are essential but not sufficient in developing healthy leaders. Consequently, we have many "disconnections" in our leaders today.

   The author attended a meeting of a local church's leadership team. The senior pastor expressed his desire for more "leadership training" in the church. The team discussed how to do this. Then one of the team members offered to begin teaching a course on New Testament survey. They all agreed this was a good idea and moved on to the next subject – the issue of "leadership development" had been successfully addressed!

   Years ago a young man said to the author, "I've spent the last seven years of my life and a huge sum of money in gaining an advanced religious education. Now I've finally graduated from university with a higher degree. In the eyes of the religious world I'm equipped, I'm qualified, I'm ready to go. But, in reality, I don't know where to go, what to do when I get there or how to do it!" This young man had graduated from quite a good Christian university, but he had a long way to go in being built as a leader. Like many leaders, he had some strong competencies in certain areas, but no overall context for those competencies, and huge lacks in some of the main areas of the Christian life!

In a recent poll conducted by Tyndale House Publishers, 80% of ministry graduates had left the pastorate in the first five years of their ministries.

Why do we have to continue doing it the same way? We don't!

As necessary as competency development is, it is not sufficient to ensure that the leader's life will result in truly positive influence or an enduring legacy (cf. Eccl. 1:16-18; 12:12). Many leaders may accomplish much but never amount to much!

According to Robert Clinton, over 70 percent of leaders who successfully climb the ladder of leadership influence do not finish well. Some dramatically fail, precipitating public scandal, while the majority of leaders who lose their influence just fade quietly into obscurity. They fall short because in their outwardly successful lives there is a disconnection between the development of leadership competencies and the development of leadership character. The lack of character is a frequent cause for leaders failing to fulfill their true potential; and this lack of character can be traced to a lack of Christ and community in the lives of the leaders.

Significantly, a recent 14-nation research project[30] found that the prime reasons for early and painful return from missionary service (in both older and younger sending countries) were not related to inadequate formal training in missions. The project found that the prime causes were clustered around issues related to spirituality, character and relationships in the life of the missionary. In other words, it is usually not a lack of competencies that undermines missionaries; it is inadequacies that occur in the other areas that are to blame. These are areas frequently not addressed in prepa-

---

[30] William Taylor (ed.). (2000). *Global Missiology for the 21st Century*. Grand Rapids, MI: Baker Book House, p. 489.

ration – Christ, community and character (no doubt calling was not specifically addressed by the research or else we suspect it would have shown up, too).

2. The more innovative academic institutions that recognize the need for character or spiritual life in their students will often add specific instruction on these subjects to their curriculum. However, character and spiritual life are not effectively developed through courses. A course on character, for example, will often not build character but rather competencies – the student will now be enabled to talk *about* character to others; this does not necessarily mean that he will actually possess it! Similarly, knowing *about* spiritual formation, as the result of successfully completing a course, does not guarantee that an emerging leader actually walks in abiding union with Christ.

The following is from an article by Vigen Guroian:

> The great Jewish philosopher Martin Buber tells the story of how he fell into "the fatal mistake of giving instruction in ethics" by presenting ethics as formal rules and principles. Buber discovered that very little of this kind of education gets "transformed into character-building substance." In his little gem of moral and educational philosophy, an essay appropriately entitled *The Education of Character*, Buber recalls: "I try to explain to my pupils that envy is despicable, and at once I feel the secret resistance of those who are poorer than their comrades. I try to explain that it is wicked to bully the weak, and at once I see a suppressed smile on the lips of the strong. I try to explain that lying destroys life, and something frightful happens: the worst habitual liar of the class produces a brilliant essay on the destructive power of lying."

> Mere instruction in morality is not sufficient to nurture the virtues. It might even backfire, especially when the presentation is heavily exhortative and the pupil's will is coerced.

Paul referred to this in Romans 7:

What shall we say, then? Is the law sin? Certainly not! Indeed I would not have known what sin was except through the law. For I would not have known what coveting really was if the law had not said, "Do not covet." But sin, seizing the opportunity afforded by the commandment, produced in me every kind of covetous desire. For apart from law, sin is dead. Once I was alive apart from law; but when the commandment came, sin sprang to life and I died. I found that the very commandment that was intended to bring life actually brought death. (Rom. 7:7-10)

Apart from the transforming grace of God, knowledge of holiness and character will only bring condemnation – we will know more about how we should be living but are not.[31]

3. The ConneXions model can be used as a prescriptive, descriptive, diagnostic and evaluative tool.

    Prescriptive: The model establishes a balanced agenda for leader development. If we are going to build leaders, we know the areas of life that need to be addressed. Before we start building something, we will usually have a blueprint of some kind – a picture of our goal (Luke 14:28). In Christian leader development, we must first have the right goal. The model thus gives us a conceptual framework within which we can work on building leaders. All five areas must be addressed effectively.

    Descriptive: We can look at our own lives or someone else's and understand who they are, where they're at, and where they need to go next. The model gives us a conceptual framework within which we can understand a leader.

---

[31] Please see *The Christian and the Law* by Malcolm Webber for more on this.

Diagnostic: When there is a problem, this model becomes a lens through which we can view a life or ministry and identify the weaknesses or problems that need to be addressed, and form a cohesive plan to address them.

Evaluative: This model provides a clear basis for holistic evaluation. Such an evaluation will be most effective when it combines self-evaluation with community-integrated evaluation.

4. A "healthy" leader is not a "perfect" leader; no one will ever be perfect in any of the 5Cs. A healthy leader is one who is *strong* and *growing* in the 5Cs.

   The fact that a leader is growing, by itself is not enough. If a leader is distinctly weak in any of the 5Cs, he is, by definition, a disconnected, unhealthy leader; he is not healthy simply because he is growing – although, he may, indeed, be growing toward health. In a parallel, a physically sick man is not immediately healthy simply because his sickness is improving.

   On the other hand, a leader should not be described as "healthy" simply because he is strong in all 5Cs; he needs also to be growing. Continual growth is a core and indispensable component of being healthy:

   > ...*speaking the truth in love, we will in all things grow up into him who is the Head, that is, Christ. From him the whole body, joined and held together by every supporting ligament, grows and builds itself up in love, as each part does its work. (Eph. 4:15-16)*

   > *All over the world this gospel is bearing fruit and growing, just as it has been doing among you since the day you heard it and understood God's grace in all its truth. (Col. 1:6)*

And we pray this in order that you may live a life worthy of the Lord and may please him in every way: bearing fruit in every good work, growing in the knowledge of God, being strengthened with all power according to his glorious might so that you may have great endurance and patience, and joyfully giving thanks to the Father, who has qualified you to share in the inheritance of the saints in the kingdom of light. (Col. 1:10-12)

So then, just as you received Christ Jesus as Lord, continue to live in him, rooted and built up in him, strengthened in the faith as you were taught, and overflowing with thankfulness. (Col. 2:6-7)

We ought always to thank God for you, brothers, and rightly so, because your faith is growing more and more, and the love every one of you has for each other is increasing. (2 Thess. 1:3)

2 Peter 1:5-11 urges believers, in reference to a number of qualities, to add to what they have already become – those who are increasing in these qualities will be fruitful in the knowledge of Christ, foresighted, protected from stumbling, supplied with ongoing kingdom life and authority in union with Christ.

Paul, in Philippians 3:12-16, does not rest on what he has already attained or apprehended; he presses on for more in Christ. In fact, his depiction of maturity is of one who continually presses onward.

Thus, a healthy leader is continually growing:

- This is a biblical idea, as noted above.
- This is realistic. Before the resurrection, no one will ever be perfect. But we do all need to be continually growing.

127

- This protects us from perfectionism with all its attendant guilt and condemnation on one hand (when you know you're not perfect), and pride and self-reliance on the other (when you think you are perfect).
- This aids us in evaluating leaders. Perfection is unobtainable, and "maturity" can even be difficult to define. However, in the context of two points in time we can assess more concretely the progress of a leader. For example, "Describe three or more ways you have grown in the past six months as a result of your commitment to live in the accountability of community..."

5. The 5C model works in every area of life and leadership.

    For example, a father needs to work on all five areas of his life to be effective and properly fruitful in his ministry of leadership to his family.

    The model is actually a model of a holistic Christian life, generally speaking.

6. The 5Cs should not be approached sequentially, but concurrently. If you wait until you've fully matured in one before you move to the next, you'll never move! You should work on all of them at the same time. Nevertheless, the two broad contexts of Christ and Community need to be the first elements in place; they have priority.

    The best design is use a spiral pattern, working on all 5Cs, going deeper and deeper with them all.

7. As the following table illustrates, all five elements have counterfeits. These counterfeits have the appearance of the genuine things; in reality they are mere outward forms, lacking legitimate substance.

Genuine	Counterfeit
Christ	Religion
Community	Ritual/Church attendance
Character	Hypocrisy/Self-righteousness
Calling	Ambition
Competencies	Empty credentials/Big talk

8. Certain cultures may have predispositions towards particular weaknesses or imbalance regarding these five elements. For example, in the United States, community is probably the weakest element in the lives of many Christian leaders. In certain African and Asian cultures, clarity regarding calling is the weakest link.

9. This model should also be used a basis for effective leader care. The leader needs nurture in all five areas.

10. Thus, an effective, healthy Christian leader is a man or woman who knows God, was formed and lives in supportive and accountable community, has strong character, knows the purpose of God and presents it with credibility, clarity and passion, and has the necessary gifts, skills and knowledge to lead the people in the accomplishment of this purpose – and is continually growing in all five areas.

> *And this is my prayer: that your love may abound more and more in knowledge and depth of insight, so that you may be able to discern what is best and may be pure and blameless until the day of Christ, filled with the fruit of righteousness that comes through Jesus Christ – to the glory and praise of God. (Phil. 1:9-11)*

chapter 8

The Sixth "C"

A mature leader continues his leadership through others. The sixth "C" is Continuance.

The ultimate test of a leader is not whether he makes smart decisions and takes effective action in the short term, but whether he teaches others to be leaders and builds an organization that can continue to be healthy and to thrive when he is not around.

The effective leader is not only a continuous learner himself; he must also be a continuous teacher and builder of others. He must pass along what he has learned to others who will then pass their learning along to others.

Jesus built His disciples who then turned the world upside down. Look at Jesus' desire:

> *Most assuredly, I say to you, he who believes in Me, the works that I do he will do also; and greater works than these he will do, because I go to My Father. (John 14:12, NKJV)*

This is the desire of the truly great leader: to build other leaders who will entirely outdo him! His goal is to raise up leaders who will stand on his shoulders and then raise up more leaders who will stand on their shoulders and so forth.

David was a mighty warrior who built other warriors. The Bible contains many examples of leaders who built leaders. Paul built leaders who built leaders:

And the things you have heard me say in the presence of many witnesses entrust to reliable men who will also be qualified to teach others. (2 Tim. 2:2)

Effective leaders personally invest time and spiritual and emotional energy in building others. Moreover, they expect the leaders they build to do the same.

This, then, is the sixth characteristic of a healthy leader: an effective leader builds other leaders![32]

---

[32] Please see *Building Leaders: SpiritBuilt Leadership 4* by Malcolm Webber for more on this.

chapter 9

Indicators of the 5Cs with Their Biblical Basis

According to our "ConneXions" Model, a healthy Christian leader knows God (Christ), was formed and lives in supportive and accountable community (Community), has integrity (Character), knows the purpose of God and presents it with clarity, passion and credibility (Calling), and has the capacity to think and act effectively in leading the people in the accomplishment of this purpose (Competencies) – and he is continually growing in all five areas (the "5Cs").

These areas of deep change in a leader's life are nurtured through the "Four Dynamics of Transformation" (the "4Ds"):

- **Spiritual Dynamics** – including prayer, worship, reflection, meditation in the Word;
- **Relational Dynamics** – including encouragement, accountability, examples, mentors, coaches;
- **Experiential Dynamics** – including learning by doing, challenging assignments, and pressure;
- **Instructional Dynamics** – the teaching of the Word of God in an engaging and interactive way, integrating doctrine into the context of life, experiences and relationships.

When all 4Ds are strongly present in a training design, spiritual life is nurtured, relational capacities are strengthened, character is developed, calling is clarified and deep capacities to think and act are built.

The following specific indicators for each of the 5Cs provide:

- A clear path for evaluating one's own leadership. (For an online evaluation tool that uses this model – the 5C Checkpoint tool – please go to: www.5CCheckpoint.com)
- A clear goal for designing training.
- A clear way to evaluate training – both the training itself and its effectiveness.
- As a basis for prayer for emerging and existing leaders.

"Christ" refers to the leader's spiritual life. Jesus' first great commandment is to: "Love the Lord your God with all your heart and with all your soul and with all your mind and with all your strength." (Mark 12:30).

A leader who is strong in Christ:

1. Trusts Jesus for his eternal life. (Mark 16:16; John 17:3; 20:31; Rom. 3:28; Gal. 2:16)
2. Receives and is secure in Christ's love. (John 15:10; 17:26; 1 John 4:16-18)
3. Recognizes that without Christ he can do nothing of eternal value. (John 15:5)
4. Enjoys continual inward fellowship with Jesus by His Holy Spirit and is consistently guided by Him. (John 14:21-23; 17:3; Rom. 8:14; 2 Cor. 3:18; Eph. 5:18; Phil. 2:1; 1 John 1:3)
5. Surrenders his life to Jesus, putting His Kingdom before his own personal desires and agendas, and submits to Jesus' authority for his beliefs and decisions. (Matt. 6:33; 7:13-14, 21; Rom. 10:9; 12:1-2; Rev. 14:4)
6. He turns more deeply to God in times of difficulty and suffering, drawing peace and strength from Him. (2 Cor. 1:3-11; 12:1-10; 2 Thess. 3:5; Heb. 4:16; 1 Pet. 1:6-9; 4:12-19)
7. Enjoys the Presence of God. (John 17:3; 1 John 1:1-3)
8. Has a healthy fear of God. (1 John 4:18; Rom. 8:15; Heb. 2:14-15; Rom. 11:20-22; 2 Cor. 5:9-11; Phil. 2:12-13; Heb. 4:1; 12:28-29; 1 Pet. 1:17; 2:17; Rev. 19:5)

9. Avoids idols and every form of the occult. (Ex. 20:3-4; Deut. 18:9-13; 1 Cor. 10:14-22; Gal. 5:20)

10. Passionately worships God. (John 4:23-24)

11. Occasionally withdraws from people and responsibilities to spend time alone with God. (Luke 4:1-2, 42-44; 5:15-16; 6:12; 9:18, 28; 11:1-2; 22:39-40; Eph. 5:19-20; Col. 3:16; Matt. 6:1-18; Ex. 20:8-11; Mark 6:31)

12. Prays consistently. (Matt. 6:6-13; 7:7-11; Mark 14:38; Eph. 6:18; 1 Thess. 5:17)

13. Has his prayers answered. (John 15:7; Jam. 5:16; 1 John 5:14-15)

14. Deliberately takes up his cross daily, treating the old life as dead, and walking in new life in Christ. (Rom. 6; Eph. 4:22-24; Col. 3:9-10)

15. Is engaged in spiritual warfare, resisting the enemy. (Luke 10:19; Eph. 4:27; 6:10-12; Jam. 4:7; 1 Pet. 5:8-9)

16. Talks about Jesus in day-to-day conversation. (Col. 4:5-6; Philemon 6; 1 Pet. 3:15)

17. Demonstrates in his attitudes, words and actions that he trusts Jesus in his everyday life. (Matt. 6:25-34; 2 Tim. 4:18; Jam. 2:14-16)

18. Lives for eternal reward, not blessing in this life. (Matt. 6:19-24; Acts 20:24; 2 Cor. 4:18; Phil. 1:21-23)

19. Loves the Word of God. (Ps. 119:97, 127, 165, 167)

20. Believes that the Bible is the true Word of God. (Ps. 12:6; 119:86, 160; John 17:17; 1 Thess. 2:13; 2 Tim. 3:16; 2 Pet. 1:20-21)

21. Meditates regularly on God's Word. (Ps. 1:1-3; Rom. 12:2; Eph. 5:26)

22. Relies on the Holy Spirit to illuminate the Word of God. (John 16:13; 1 Cor. 2:10-13)

23. Submits to the biblical revelation as the final authority on every subject it addresses. (Is. 8:20; Matt. 24:35; John 10:35; Gal. 1:8)

24. Looks to the Word of God for direction and answers to his daily questions. (Josh. 1:8; Ps. 1:1-3; Matt. 4:4; 7:24; Jam. 1:22)

25. Carefully guards his own doctrine and that of those for whom he is responsible. (Acts 20:28; 1 Cor. 15:1-2; 1 Tim. 3:9; 4:16; 2 Tim. 1:13-14; 3:14-17; 4:5; Tit. 1:9; 1 John 2:24-25; 2 John 9)

26. Is not content with a purely academic knowledge of the Scriptures, but seeks to experience and share its life-transforming power. (Ps. 119:11; Prov. 4:20-22; John 5:39-40; 6:63; Eph. 5:25-27; 1 Thess. 2:13; 2 Tim. 3:16-17; Jam. 1:18; 1 Pet. 1:23; 1 John 2:14)

"Community" refers to the leader's relationships with others. Jesus' second great commandment is to: "Love your neighbor as yourself" (Mark 12:31). This includes four kinds of relationship – in marriage and family, in the church, with other leaders, and with people in the world.

A leader who is strong in Community:

1. Loves others as himself, treating them as he would like to be treated. (Matt. 7:12; 22:39; Rom. 13:8-10; 2 Pet. 1:7; 1 John 3:16-18)

2. Is not self-seeking, considering the good of others before his own. (Rom. 12:10; 15:1; 1 Cor. 13:5; 2 Cor. 11:29; Phil. 2:3-11)

3. Forgives those who have wronged him, keeping no record of wrongs; is not resentful. He blesses those who curse him, turning the other cheek rather than defending himself. (Ex. 20:13; Matt. 5:10-12, 21-26, 38-41; 6:14-15; 18:21-35; Rom. 12:17-21; 1 Cor. 6:7; 13:5; Eph. 4:32; Col. 3:13)

4. Is merciful, kind and courteous. (Matt. 5:7; 1 Cor. 13:4; Gal. 5:22; 2 Tim. 2:24)

5. Gives affirmation and support to strengthen others. (1 Cor. 16:17-18; 2 Tim. 1:16; Eph. 4:29; 5:4; Col. 3:16; 1 Thess. 5:11; Jam. 3)

6. Prays for others. (Eph. 6:18-20; Jam. 5:16)

7. Is a generous giver and acts hospitably to all, especially the stranger and the needy. (Prov. 14:31; Matt. 6:1-4; Acts 20:35; 2 Cor. 8:9; 9:7; Eph. 4:28; 1 Tim. 6:17-19; Rom. 12:13; 1 Thess. 5:14; 1 Tim. 3:2; Jam. 1:27)

8. Is unprejudiced and inclusive toward others. (Rom. 12:16; 14:1; Gal. 5:20, 22; Phil. 2:2-3)

9. Is good at working with different people, recognizing and adjusting to their various backgrounds, cultures and personalities. (1 Cor. 12:21-22; Gal. 3:28)

10. Thinks and acts interdependently with others. (Prov. 15:22; 1 Cor. 12; Eph. 4:1-16)

11. Allows other believers the freedom to determine their own convictions on minor issues. (Rom. 14; 1 Cor. 8:1-13)

12. Does not engage in malicious talk or gossip. (2 Cor. 12:20; Eph. 4:31)

13. Does not start unnecessary conflict; when conflict occurs, he prayerfully and actively seeks to resolve it, working always for unity. (Matt. 5:9; Rom. 14:19; Gal. 5:20, 22; Eph. 4:1-4)

14. Meets regularly with other believers to fellowship, worship, share the communion of the bread and cup, pray and study the Scriptures. (Acts 2:42; 1 Cor. 11:23-34; 14:26; Heb. 10:25)

15. Shares his life as well as his teaching with those to whom he ministers. (Mark 3:14; 2 Tim. 3:10)

16. Leads and manages his own family well. (1 Tim. 3:5, 12)

17. Treats his spouse, parents, children and/or siblings with self-giving love and respect. (Ex. 20:12; Eph. 5:22-33; 6:1-3; Col. 3:18-21; 1 Tim. 3:4-5; Tit. 1:6; 1 Pet. 3:1-7)

18. Fulfills his vocational responsibilities faithfully and effectively, obeying his leaders from the heart and not with "eye-service." If he is the leader, he genuinely cares for his followers. (1 Tim. 3:5, 15; 5:17; 1 Pet. 5:2; Eph. 6:5-9; Col. 3:22 – 4:1)

19. Is a healthy follower. (Rom. 13:1; Heb. 13:17)

20. Graciously shares ideas and feedback with those in appropriate authority and ultimately submits to them from the heart, with respect, whether or not he agrees (unless it involves disobedience to God). (Gen. 33; Ruth 1:16-17; Esther 3 – 7; Neh. 2:3-8; Dan. 1; Rom. 13:1-7; 1 Thess. 5:12-13; Heb. 13:17; Acts 5:29)

21. Seeks feedback and accepts healthy correction without self-justification, self-pity or complaint. (Prov. 9:8-9; 2 Cor. 7:10; Phil. 2:14)

22. Questions others when appropriate and gives correction discreetly and tactfully. (1 Tim. 5:1-2; Philemon)

Emotional Intelligence:

23. Is self-aware, knowing how he feels and how his emotions and actions affect the people around him. (Prov. 21:2; Rom. 12:3; Gal. 6:3)
24. Manages his own emotions well. (Prov. 15:28; 1 Cor. 9:24-27; Phil. 4:8-9; Tit. 1:8; Heb. 4:15; Jam. 3:2)
25. Is aware of how others feel. (Matt. 9:36; Rom. 12:15; 1 Pet. 3:8; 1 John 3:17)
26. Is able to manage the emotions of others. (Prov. 12:18; 17:2; Gal. 5:19-23)

"Character" refers to the leader's personal integrity.

A leader who is strong in Character:

1. Is committed to obeying the Bible. (Matt. 7:24-27; Acts 20:27; 2 Tim. 3:16-17; Jam. 2:14-26)
2. Is joyful – thankful to God and positive toward life. (Rom. 12:12; 1 Cor. 13:6-7; Gal. 5:22; Eph. 5:20; Col. 3:15; 1 Thess. 5:16; Tit. 1:8)
3. Is truthful and honest; not lying, cheating or stealing. He pursues what is right above what is expedient or popular. (Ex. 20:15-16; Matt. 5:8; Eph. 4:25, 28; Col. 3:9)
4. Is faithful and trustworthy, keeping confidences and following through on responsibilities and commitments. (Prov. 25:13; Matt. 5:33-37; 2 Cor. 1:18; 8:11; Gal. 5:22; 1 Tim. 3:11; Jam. 5:12)
5. Is humble – not overbearing, rude, proud or boastful. Doesn't let power or status go to his head. (Matt. 5:3-5; 1 Cor. 13:4-5; Eph. 4:2; 1 Pet. 5:5-6)
6. Exhibits patience and self-control; is not impulsive. (Gal. 5:23; 1 Tim. 3:2-3; Tit. 1:7; 2 Pet. 1:6)

7. Perseveres during adversity, without complaining or arguing, with hope resting in God. (2 Cor. 1:9-10; Phil. 2:14; 2 Tim. 4:5; Jam. 5:10-11; 2 Pet. 1:6)

8. Is resilient, dealing well with setbacks and bouncing back from failure or defeat. (Prov. 24:16; Rom. 8:31-39; 1 Pet. 1:6-7)

9. Is tenacious, without being stubborn or unteachable. (2 Cor. 4:16-17; Heb. 13:5-6)

10. Is flexible, good at varying his approach with the situation. Takes ideas different from his own seriously, and occasionally changes his mind. (Prov. 9:8-9; Ex. 18:23-24)

11. Is slow to anger, responding proactively rather than reactively. (1 Cor. 13:5; 1 Tim. 3:2-3)

12. Is not given to overeating, drunkenness or addictions. (Gal. 5:21; Prov. 23:2; Eph. 5:18; 1 Tim. 3:3; Tit. 1:7; 2:3)

13. Refrains from lust, sexual immorality, pornography, profanity, immodesty and all forms of impurity. (Ex. 20:14; Matt. 5:27-30; Rom. 13:13; 1 Cor. 6:13-20; Gal. 5:19-21; Eph. 5:3; Col. 3:5; 1 Tim. 5:2; 1 Pet. 3:3-5; 4:2)

14. Is not greedy, covetous, jealous or envious but is content with what he has. (Ex. 20:17; 1 Cor. 13:4; Gal. 5:20-21; 1 Tim. 6:6-10; Prov. 30:8; Acts 20:33-35; Eph. 5:3; 1 Tim. 3:3; Tit. 1:7; 1 Pet. 5:2)

15. Stewards resources well, exercises self-control financially, and is not irresponsible with debt. Does not gamble. (Prov. 13:11; 22:7; Rom. 13:8)

16. Takes responsibility for his own physical care, well-being and fitness. (1 Cor. 6:20; 1 Tim. 4:8)

17. Guards himself. Avoids spreading himself too thin, dealing well with the tensions between work and family. (1 Tim. 4:6; 1 Cor. 9:25; Eph. 5:16; 1 Tim. 3:2; 2 Pet. 1:6)

18. Does not take advantage of his authority, using it for personal gain. (Acts 20:30; 2 Cor. 7:2; 12:14-18; Phil. 2:6; 1 Pet. 5:3)

19. Recognizes others for their accomplishments without personally taking the credit. (Rom. 16:3-4, 6-7; 2 Cor. 1:11)

20. Does not blame others when things go wrong, but takes responsibility for his own decisions and actions. (Gen. 3:12; Phil. 2:14)

21. Is appropriately transparent, willing to admit ignorance or struggles. Doesn't hide mistakes. (Luke 22:42; 2 Cor. 1:8-11; 12:1-10; Jam. 5:16; 1 John 1:8-10)
22. Has a good reputation. (1 Thess. 4:12; 1 Tim. 3:7; 1 Pet. 3:16)

"Calling" refers to the leader's vision and purpose in God. Calling includes six core realities:

- God does everything with clear purpose.
- Everyone has individual purpose given by God.
- God calls certain individuals to be organizational leaders. They must be clear about their personal calling.
- Churches and ministries have a corporate calling from God.
- Our personal callings integrate with the corporate calling of our church or ministry.
- Leadership primarily means "movement" so every leader must understand and communicate the vision God has for those whom he leads.

A leader who is strong in Calling:

1. Serves God zealously out of a strong sense of destiny and divine purpose. (Jer. 1:5; Rom. 12:11; 2 Tim. 1:9)
2. Has a passion for the highest, always striving to grow, to solve, to build, to overcome – always pressing on to fulfill God's purposes, with hope for the future, believing that things can be improved and problems can be solved, and seizing new opportunities. (Phil. 3:12-14)
3. Faces reality, in order to deal with the real problems and the real opportunities. (Mark 7:5-8)
4. Engages deeply with the people and world around him. (Matt. 9:36; Luke 19:41-44; Acts 17:16; Rom. 12:15; 2 Cor. 11:28-29)
5. Has a vision that is not limited to his own local community, but extends to God's work in the nations. (Acts 1:8; Col. 1:23; Is. 49:6)
6. Has an increasingly-clear understanding of his own motivated abilities and God's will for his life. (Rom. 12:2; Phil. 1:9-10)

7. Stays focused in his calling, setting priorities well, distinguishing clearly between important and unimportant tasks, and avoiding the distractions of other opportunities. (Col. 4:17; 2 Tim. 4:5, 10)

8. Has a vision that comes from God and not his own ambition. (Jer. 14:14; 23:16; Acts 20:30; Gal. 5:20; Jam. 3:14; 4:13-16)

9. Is motivated by vision from God rather than the mere requirements of position. (1 Pet. 5:2)

10. Seeks the approval of God for his ministry rather than the approval of people. (Matt. 6:1-2, 5, 16; 23:5-12)

11. Does not compromise his calling out of fear, or pressure from others. (Jer. 1:4-8; Matt. 10:32-33; Luke 14:26; Acts 20:18-24; Phil. 1:14, 27-28; 1 Tim. 4:12-14; 2 Tim. 1:6-7)

12. Regularly and prayerfully reflects on his life, recognizing that God uses people, events and circumstances to prepare him for his ministry. (Rom. 8:28; Eph. 1:11)

13. Exercises the giftings of God, while seeking to grow in them. (Rom. 12:3-8; 1 Pet. 4:10-11)

14. Loves to learn and grow, intentionally exploring a variety of ministry opportunities, including ones that require him to stretch. (Prov. 8:17; 15:14; 18:15; 19:8, 20; 23:12; Eph. 4:15-16)

15. Seeks out relationships with mature believers and leaders to learn from them. (Rom. 16:13; 2 Tim. 3:14)

16. Pursues further learning of the Word of God. (Ps. 119; Matt. 15:6, 9; Heb. 5:11-14)

17. Evaluates the fruitfulness of his ministry in order to discern and confirm his calling. (2 Cor. 13:5)

18. Serves at a level of authority appropriate to his gifting, maturity and favor. (Luke 16:10, 12; Rom. 12:3; 2 Cor. 10:12-18)

19. Takes initiative, not waiting to be asked to act or take responsibility. (Prov. 6:6-8; 30:27; Matt. 25:14-30)

20. Selflessly pursues his own calling as a means to build up the church and not to promote himself. Does not exploit or use people for his own ambition. (Matt. 20:25-28; 1 Cor. 9:19-23; Eph. 4:12; Phil. 1:24-25)

21. Possesses spiritual authority that is recognized by others. (Matt. 9:8; Acts 16:2; 2 Cor. 10:18)
22. Casts a compelling vision for the future. (1 Pet. 3:15)
23. Inspires others to grow and take action to fulfill their calling from God. (Rom. 15:14; Eph. 4:12, 16)

"Competencies" refers to the leader's capacities to think and act. The following "master competencies" cover a wide range of thinking and acting capacities, and provide the leader the ability to understand and then respond well to the challenges and opportunities of life and ministry.

A leader who is strong in Competencies:

THINKING

Thinking holistically:
1. Sees the big picture, recognizing how each part relates to the whole. (1 Cor. 3:1-10; Eph. 4:16)
2. Is aware of the broad external environment, spotting problems, opportunities and trends early on. (1 Chron. 12:32; Matt. 16:3; Eph. 5:16)
3. Can create order out of large quantities of information. (Eccl. 12:9; Matt. 13:37-40; Gal. 5:14)

Embracing ambiguity:
4. Embraces ambiguity and uncertainty, recognizing the opportunities they create. (Prov. 26:4-5; Phil. 2:12-13)

Integrating Science and Art:
5. Thinks creatively, consistently generating new and innovative ideas, appropriately challenging the status quo and willing to take risks. (Ex. 35:31-32; Matt. 13:52; 14:29; Acts 10:19-21, 25-29; Eph. 2:10)
6. Is good at systematic and critical analysis, probing beneath the surface. (1 Sam. 16:7; 1 Kings 3:16-28; 4:29-34; John 7:24; Acts 15:13-21; Col. 2:23)

7. Thinking about thinking:
8. Continually reflects and evaluates. (Prov. 14:15; Eph. 5:15; Gal. 6:4)

Learning from mistakes:
9. Learns from failure and mistakes. (Prov. 14:4; 26:11-12; Luke 22:32; 1 Cor. 10:11; 1 John 1:9-10)

ACTING

Building leaders:
10. Identifies emerging leaders. (Mark 3:14; Acts 16:1-2)
11. Personally builds leaders, coaching and mentoring them. (Mark 3:14-15; 2 Tim. 3:10-17)
12. Gives challenging assignments to those he is building. (Gen. 22:1-2; Matt. 10:5-10; 28:18-20; John 6:5-6; 2 Cor. 2:9; 8:8)
13. Cares for the leaders around him. (Phil. 2:25; 4:10-19; 1 Corinthians 16:15-18; 2 Cor. 7:5-7; 2 Tim. 1:16-18)

Team building:
14. Is a good team builder, bringing together people with different personalities and strengths. (Rom. 12:3-8; 1 Cor. 12)
15. Empowers others, giving them both responsibility and authority, along with much encouragement. (Matt. 10:1-20; 1 Tim. 1:3; 4:12)
16. Provides accountability for others with regular and constructive feedback. (Matt. 6:30; Luke 9:10; 10:17-20; Acts 14:27; 15:4, 12; 21:19)
17. Recognizes and rewards others for their work, celebrating accomplishments. (Ex. 12:42; Esther 9:26-28; Acts 11:18; 1 Thess. 5:12-13)

Leading change:
18. Leads change successfully. (Ex. 3:8; 15:13, 17; Num. 27:15-17; Neh. 2:17-18; Matt. 28:19-20; Acts 26:16-18; Rom. 12:1-2; Col. 1:13; 1 Pet. 2:9)
19. Understands the culture of the organization (shared beliefs, values, attitudes, actions, language) and intentionally shapes it in the right direction. (Eph. 4:16)
20. Is able to positively influence people over whom he has no direct positional authority. (Luke 2:46-52; Acts 9:20-22; 2 Cor. 3:1-2)

Strategizing:
21. Translates the broad vision into specific strategies. (Mark 16:15; Acts 1:8)
22. Creates actionable goals, plans, structures and systems. (Ex. 18:13-26; 2 Chron. 3; Acts 6:1-6; 1 Cor. 16:1-4)

Managing:
23. Manages his own life wisely, including his time. (Eph. 5:16; Col. 4:5)
24. Manages people well. (Ex. 18:13-26; Neh. 3; Acts 6:1-7)
25. Effectively mobilizes resources, including finances. (1 Chron. 29:1-9; 2 Cor. 8-9)
26. Stewards organizational resources responsibly. (Prov. 31:10-31; Matt. 25:14-29)
27. Understands and implements healthy organizational governance. (Acts 14:23; 15:2; Tit. 1:5; 1 Pet. 5:1)
28. Possesses the necessary knowledge and skills for his particular role and responsibilities. (Prov. 22:29)

Decision making:
29. Is decisive, analyzing choices and making timely decisions, without unnecessary delay. (Josh. 24:15; Ps. 119:60; 1 Kings 18:21; Matt. 21:28-32; Gal. 2:4-5, 11-14; Rev. 3:15-16)
30. Involves others in decision-making as appropriate. (Ex. 18:13-26; Acts 6:1-6; 15:1-21, 25)

Problem solving:

31. Deals with problems early, before they become out of control. (Matt. 5:25; Acts 15:1-31; Gal. 1:6-9)
32. Defines problems accurately, getting to the heart of the issue. (Acts 8:18-25; 9:26-30; 13:5-12; 16:16-18; Rom. 14)

Communicating:

33. Communicates with clarity. (Mark 1:22; Luke 2:47; 4:22, 32; 1 Cor. 14:8; Col. 4:4)
34. Communicates with passion. (Is. 58:1; Jer. 20:9; Hos. 8:1; Amos 3:8; Acts 4:20; 14:14-18; 20:30-31; 1 Cor. 9:16; 2 Cor. 2:4; Phil. 3:18)
35. Communicates with credibility. (Acts 17:2; 18:4; Eph. 6:19; Col. 4:6; 1 Tim. 4:11-16; 1 Pet. 3:15)
36. Actively listens to others. (Prov. 18:13; Jam. 1:19)

Negotiation:

37. Negotiates well, trading-off and working towards solutions that are best for everyone. (Acts 15:36-41; Gal. 2:9-10; 1 Cor. 10:23-24)

Networking:

38. Networks with others, initiating and nurturing numerous positive relationships. (Rom. 16; Col. 4:7-17)
39. Builds relational networks with those outside his own group. (Acts 10; 18:24-26; 19:1-7; Rom. 14; Eph. 4:1-6)

Leading meetings:

40. Leads meetings effectively, creating opportunities for participation while maintaining focus. (Acts 15:14-30; 1 Cor. 14)

41. Has extensive and accurate knowledge of the Bible. (1 Tim. 1:7; 2 Tim. 2:2)
42. Interprets the Scriptures soundly. (2 Tim. 2:15; Tit. 2:8)
43. Is knowledgeable about the church's history and its established and historically-accepted doctrine. (1 Tim. 4:6; 2 Tim. 1:5, 13; Tit. 1:9)
44. Teaches the Word of God in a positive and engaging way. (Phil. 1:7; 1 Tim. 1:3; 4:1-3; 2 Tim. 4:2; Tit. 1:9)
45. Is practical and relevant in his teaching. (1 Tim. 1:5; 4:7; Tit. 2:1-2)
46. Gently and effectively corrects those who are in doctrinal error, including the cults. (Phil. 1:7; 2 Tim. 2:16-18, 24-26; 4:2; Tit. 1:9; Jude 3)
47. Actively engaged and effective in Christian ministry work, including leading others to Christ, discipling new believers, spiritual warfare, discerning and responding to the presence of the Holy Spirit, etc.

Books in the *SpiritBuilt Leadership* Series

by Malcolm Webber, Ph.D.

1. *Leadership.* Deals with the nature of leadership, servant leadership, and other basic leadership issues.
2. *Healthy Leaders.* Presents a simple but effective model of what constitutes a healthy Christian leader.
3. *Leading.* A study of the practices of exemplary leaders.
4. *Building Leaders.* Leaders build leaders! However, leader development is highly complex and very little understood. This book examines core principles of leader development.
5. *Leaders & Managers.* Deals with the distinctions between leaders and managers. Contains extensive worksheets.
6. *Abusive Leadership.* A must read for all Christian leaders. Reveals the true natures and sources of abusive leadership and servant leadership.
7. *Understanding Change.* Leading change is one of the most difficult leadership responsibilities. It is also one of the most important. This book is an excellent primer that will help you understand resistance to change, the change process and how to help people through change.
8. *Building Teams.* What teams are and how they best work.
9. *Understanding Organizations.* A primer on organizational structure.
10. *Women in Leadership.* A biblical study concerning this very controversial issue.
11. *Healthy Followers.* The popular conception that "everything depends on leaders" is not entirely correct. Without thoughtful and active followers, the greatest of leaders will fail. This book studies the characteristics of healthy followers and is also a great resource for team building.
12. *Listening.* Listening is one of the most important of all leadership skills. This book studies how we can be better listeners and better leaders.

Strategic Press
www.StrategicPress.org

Strategic Press is a division of Strategic Global Assistance, Inc.
www.sgai.org

513 S. Main St. Suite 2
Elkhart, IN 46516
U.S.A.

+1-844-532-3371 (LEADER-1)

CPSIA information can be obtained
at www.ICGtesting.com
Printed in the USA
LVHW082207191120
672185LV00040B/415

9 781888 810622